A Legal GUIDE TO THE INTERNET

Sixth Edition
April 2006

A Collaborative Effort
Minnesota Department of Employment and Economic Development
Merchant & Gould P.C.

ISBN 1-888404-44-2

TABLE OF CONTENTS

PREFACE

Speed is the principal characteristic of the Internet: speed of computers, speed of transactions, speed of technology adoption, speed of competition, speed of growth, speed of the transformation of industries and markets.

That speed of activity in pursuit of fast profits can often blur the focus needed to control costs which likewise can grow very quickly in the Internet environment. While electronic commerce can eliminate some old costs like fixed overhead it brings with it new costs like web design, advertising, customer service and product branding. It also brings significant questions of ownership, copyrights, privacy, contract formation, product distribution, the terms and conditions of web site use: many of which are absent from - or not as substantially present - in non-electronic methods of commerce.

This publication seeks to address some of those legal issues as costs which can be borne early in a firm's Internet activity to reduce the possibility of more substantial liability costs later. While not intended as legal advice, it will hopefully serve as a primer to businesses in framing questions and issues for discussion with their own legal counsel and other professional advisors.

The Internet is an area requiring both broad and deep expertise which has been provided by our collaborator Merchant & Gould. At the firm a particular note of thanks goes to Michael Cohen, Gregory Golla, and William Schultz, for preparing these materials.

An electronic version of this publication, with periodic updates, will appear both at the web site of the Minnesota Department of Employment and Economic Development at www.mnsbao.com and at the web site of Merchant & Gould at www.merchant-gould.com.

Charles A. Schaffer
Minnesota Small Business Assistance Office
Minnesota Department of Employment and Economic Development

DISCLAIMER

This Guide is designed to alert Minnesota companies, employers and residents to issues which commonly arise in conjunction with operating on the Internet. It should be used only as a guide and not as a definitive source to answer your legal questions. Consultation with legal counsel is advised as you encounter situations with respect to your dealings on the Internet which you must address. We hope that this Guide will raise questions and familiarize you with frequently arising Internet law issues so that you will know when to seek professional advice before an Internet decision becomes a problem.

This Guide is designed to reflect the law as it existed through April 2006. Internet law is a new and rapidly changing area of the law, and what is true today may not be true tomorrow. The materials in this Guide are intended to provide general information and should not be relied upon for specific legal advice. Legal counsel should be consulted regarding questions and issues of protection or infringement of rights, so as to avoid possible loss of rights or infringement of the rights of others. Merchant & Gould and the Minnesota Small Business Assistance Office cannot and do not assume responsibility for decisions based upon the information provided in this Guide.

INTRODUCTION

No one can question the profound impact the Internet is having on our society. The ways we communicate, conduct business, and entertain ourselves are all changing as more individuals, businesses, and organizations become members of this new electronic community. The purpose of this sixth version of the Guide is to explore some of the new legal questions fostered by the continued growth in the scope and use of the Internet. While there are clearly new and unique issues that are exclusive to the Internet, you will also find that many existing principles of law still apply.

We hope this Guide will allow anyone conducting business through the Internet to form an understanding of some basic principles of law so the readers can continue to educate themselves and/or their legal counsel. The Internet has also introduced new terms including URL's, metatags, linking, web browsers, digital signatures, etc. It is our hope that this publication will give you a basic understanding of this new jargon. Although prepared by lawyers, this Guide should not be utilized as a substitute for legal advice in the complex and evolving area of Internet law.

We were aware that as soon as the first version of this Guide was published in August 1999, some of the information would soon be outdated. Among other new developments covered by this sixth edition are domain name disputes, cases involving jurisdiction, the Supreme Court decision on peer-to-peer file sharing, liability for uploading a computer program that erased data on a company provided laptop, and trademark infringement claims based on sponsored links. Helpful Internet sites now appear at the end of the Guide. To facilitate revisions, this publication is available on Merchant & Gould's web site www.merchantgould.com as well as the web site of the Minnesota Department of Employment and Economic Development, www.mnsbao.com. If you are looking for the most current version of this Guide, please check the above web sites to see if an update has been completed. It is our sincere hope that you will find the following Guide not only informative and provocative, but useful as you enter the exciting and dynamic world of the Internet.

Michael R. Cohen
Merchant & Gould

GETTING YOUR BUSINESS STARTED ON THE INTERNET

The Internet presents a new frontier with unlimited potential. The purpose of this Guide is to ensure that legal issues are properly considered to provide individuals and businesses maximum protection with minimum liability.

This chapter outlines the initial steps towards establishing a business on the Internet. Key issues involved with these steps are identified. As these issues are identified, the reader is directed to relevant sections of this Guide for a more detailed explanation.

A business' use of the Internet varies. Simple activities such as connecting to the Internet, obtaining external e-mail capability for company employees, and setting up a basic web site are the initial steps. More complicated steps include establishing a web site that can process consumer transactions. No matter what level of involvement, a business must balance the advantages and disadvantages of entering the Internet. Even the basic steps take time and entail a certain degree of legal, security, and business risk. Therefore, venturing into the Internet and into the world of electronic commerce must make financial sense.

STARTING AND RUNNING A WEB SITE

The first step in establishing a presence on the Internet is to get connected to the external world. Businesses typically select an Internet Service Provider (ISP) with high-speed connectivity. The ISP provides a web server (computer) to host your web site and at least two domain name servers that allow users to find your web site. ISPs can be found in the phone book or at numerous web sites. When selecting an ISP, one should look at possible advancements in technology and whether the ISP will be able to provide these advancements. Businesses should be leery about entering into long-term contracts with ISPs who do not have the capability of expanding and growing with new technology. (See the section of this Guide on Contracts for a detailed explanation of what terms to look for when entering agreements). An examination of the ISP's capabilities regarding SPAM, privacy policies, and connectivity time should also be considered.

The next step is to obtain a domain name. A domain name serves as a company's business address on the Internet. One must select an appropriate name for the web site and the appropriate top-level domain name, such as ".com" or ".biz." (See the section of this Guide entitled Domain Names for a detailed explanation of the domain name system). To register a domain name, a company contacts a domain registrar to determine the availability of a certain domain name. More information on the selection and availability of domain names can be found in the next section of this Guide.

Typically, a business will hire a third party to design a web site. When hiring a web site developer, a web site development agreement should be drafted and signed by all parties involved. The web site development agreement is the central document used to define the relationship between the developer and the client. There are many variables to consider in evaluating this contract. (Issues relating to web site development agreements are discussed in the section of this Guide entitled Contracts - Web Site Development and/or Web Hosting Agreement).

Consideration should be given to the content that will be published on the site. The entire world gains access to this information. Thus, private company information must be closely examined before publication. Companies should be careful not to publish copyrighted information without consent or any content that is unlawful. It is not proper to use content from someone else just because it is on the Internet or because it does not have a copyright or trademark notice. Similarly, the background content or code of the website should not include infringing material. Establishing an Internet access policy detailing the people who have access to publish information on the company web site reduces the chances that inappropriate content reaches the public.

After the web site has been developed and approved by its owner and is ready to be seen and used by the world, it must be transferred to a server having an appropriate connection to the Internet. While some web site owners will want to operate the site in-house, many others use a third-party hosting service. The terms and conditions of using such hosting services are often the subject of a written agreement between a web site owner and a hosting service also discussed later in this Guide in the section entitled Contracts - Web Site Development and/or Web Hosting Agreement. Negotiations for web site hosting agreements tend to concentrate on anticipated uptime and response time for the site. It is also important to consider possible future transfers to a different host and compatibility with the host platform (typically UNIX, Windows, or Sun).

Increasingly, web site hosting services are offering more than just hosting of web sites. The trend in this area is toward one-stop shopping. In addition to hosting one's web site, companies are also offering to provide firms with e-mail, file transfer protocol, statistics, and other capabilities. In addition, some Internet companies are seeking to evolve into providers of complete electronic commerce solutions so that clients that wish to enter the electronic commerce arena can do so quickly and simply. Reviewing the contracts of various hosting services and asking for specifics of what is being offered is essential. However, knowing what your company needs and what is unnecessary is just as important.

There are many legal issues concerning the operation of a web site. A web site is open to the world and must be operated with caution. The following is a list of significant issues involving starting and running a web site:

- Selecting and acquiring a domain name which does not duplicate another's domain name nor infringe or dilute another's trademark;
- Obtaining a web site development agreement and hosting arrangement favorable to the business' interests;
- Respecting the copyrights of others and protecting with copyrights the business' display of its own material;
- Obtaining patent protection for any of the business' on line related inventions;
- Understanding the various government regulations of Internet commerce and ensuring that information on the business' web site is not inaccurate or misleading, false advertising, or in violation of consumer protection laws;
- Forming contracts on-line; and
- Ensuring users' privacy rights are not compromised.

LEGAL ISSUES RELATED TO USING E-MAIL AND E-VIDEO

Internet e-mail improves a business' ability to communicate with customers and other businesses allowing virtually instantaneous communications around the world. E-Video or Internet Video provides visual communications over the Internet. In order to reduce liability, businesses that use these forms of communication must take precautions to ensure that the information is secure.

Establishing an employer e-mail policy is the first step to reducing liability. Such a policy informs employees that e-mail is to be used solely for business purposes and that any e-mail transmitted or received using the company's hardware, software, or networking may be monitored. Thus, employees should be informed that business e-mail has no reasonable expectation of privacy. Restricting e-mail usage to business use reduces the number of personal messages going across the network and the potential for an unwanted lawsuit. It also increases the bandwidth of the company's Internet access, creating business efficiency.

Companies should also be aware that correspondence via e-mail might be viewed by third parties to the transactions. The Electronic Communications Protection Act makes it a federal crime to intercept an e-mail transmission during the time it is being sent from the sender to the receiver. As the time period is minimal, however, the Act may not offer adequate protection. Thus, businesses should take affirmative steps to protect online e-mail transactions. One step is to separate e-mail and other network backups onto unique servers. This allows a business to backup the network without backing up stored e-mails. However, e-mails may remain in computer memory or with the company's ISP depending on the ISP Agreement. A careful review of all agreements dealing with e-mail reduces the risk that an electronic transmission will come back to haunt the business.

Video conferencing or e-video is relatively new as compared to e-mail. However, the same issues are present. Businesses need to establish policies relating to the types of information that can be sent via the Internet.

The following are some of the issues for a business to consider relative to both its internal and external communications:

- Developing an "Employee Internet and E-mail Use Policy;"
- Preventing and avoiding liability for employee use of e-mail that harms another (e.g. defamation, sexual harassment);
- Protecting the confidentiality of e-mail with encryption and digital signatures;
- Protecting on-line materials with copyrights and respecting the copyrights of others;

- Understanding that sending e-mail into other states may create legal jurisdiction over the business in those other states or expose the business to tax liability in those states;
- Understanding that sending SPAM via e-mail may subject the business to anti-spam laws; and
- Ensuring that the business' e-mail communications with its legal counsel maintain the attorney-client privilege.

LEGAL ISSUES RELATED TO ELECTRONIC COMMERCE

As can be seen from the issues above, the movement from a purely passive or descriptive web site to a more interactive one involving the e-mail exchange of information increases the number and kind of issues with potential legal liabilities for a business. The potential for legal liability increases even more when a business begins electronic commerce, or the actual sale (or arrangements for sale) of goods or services, using the Internet. The passage of the Electronic Signature in Global and International Commerce Act (E-Signature Act) signified a leap forward with respect to electronic commerce.

The E-Signature Act was signed into law on October 1, 2000. The law provides that electronic contracts and electronic signatures are legal and enforceable just like a paper contract. Thus, clicking the "I Agree" button in an e-contract or typing the signer's name into an area designated for a signature on an online contract form accomplishes the act of signing a contract. Businesses should be aware that the transactions entered into online will have a binding effect. At the same time, companies need to be aware of their site's security and encryption measures to assure clients that hackers cannot gain access to confidential transactions. This topic will be discussed in more depth in the Security On-line and Digital Signatures section of this Guide.

Other considerations for businesses to take into account include the following:

- Federal, state, local and international authorities regulate important elements of electronic commerce like contract formation, electronic payments and consumer protection;
- Interstate electronic commerce may subject the business to lawsuits in other states;
- Interstate electronic commerce may subject the business to tax claims by other states;
- Rights and duties may arise under one or more sections of the Uniform Commercial Code, which generally controls electronic commerce;
- Unsecured or unauthenticated information may lead to breaches of corporate security or the potential loss of trade secrets;
- Intellectual property issues must be addressed to ensure the business' rights are protected and liability is not created regarding the rights of others.

DOMAIN NAMES

Computers on the Internet, called "host computers," are identified by both numbers and names. The number consists of four parts separated by periods, for example "36.152.66.39." This number is commonly referred to as the "IP Address" of the computer, pinpointing the location of that computer on the Internet, so that it may be reached by other computers.

As a string of numbers is very difficult to remember, each number has a name associated with it. This is the "domain name." Domain names have multiple levels, as shown in the corresponding diagram. All domain names contain a "top level domain," (commonly referred to as a "TLD"). The current universally recognized top level domains are listed below. These top level domains are all approved by the Internet Corporation for Assigned Names and Numbers ("ICANN"), the administrative body governing the Internet.

"us"	- reserved for U.S. citizens, residents, businesses, or organizations and federal, state, and local governments and other country codes
"com"	- typically designating a commercial company
"net"	- typically designating a networking organization
"org"	- typically designating a non-profit organization
"edu"	- designating an educational institution
"mil"	- reserved exclusively for the United States government
"int"	- used only for registering organizations established by international treaties between governments
"biz"	- reserved for businesses
"info"	- an unrestricted top level domain for information

"aero" - pertaining to the air transport industry
"coop" - designating cooperatives
"museum" - designating museums
"name" - designating individuals
"pro" - designating lawyers, accountants, and physicians

In addition, other top level domain registrations are available through companies like New.net, which operate outside of the regulatory scope of ICANN. These include "kids," "law," and "inc." Domain name registrations with these top level domains are available for purchase by the general public, but unlike the ICANN-approved top level domains, they are not fully regulated and are not recognizable by all servers.

A domain name may also have a "country code top level domain" (ccTLD) as a component. For example, "au" signifies Australia, and "uk" signifies the United Kingdom. Although most countries maintain their own country code registries, others have entered into agreements with corporations who want to market a particular country code domain. For example, the DotTV Corporation has entered into an agreement with the small nation of Tuvalu to take over the registry services for its "tv" country code domain. As a result, many United States businesses, including Motorola and Major League Baseball, now have their trademarks or trade names registered as "tv" domain names (e.g., www.motorola.tv). There are now more than 240 country code top level domains, and each country has different procedures and requirements for registration. For a list of the current country code domains and links to their registries, visit http://www.iana.org/cctld/cctld-whois.htm.

The "second level" is the main part of a domain name, and is sometimes referred to as the "domain name" in common usage. Typically, it is the second level domain that corresponds to the company's name or best-known trademark, or a description of its business. For example, second-level domains include "IBM" in the Universal Resource Locator (URL) "http://www.ibm.com," and "microsoft" in the URL "http://www.microsoft.com."

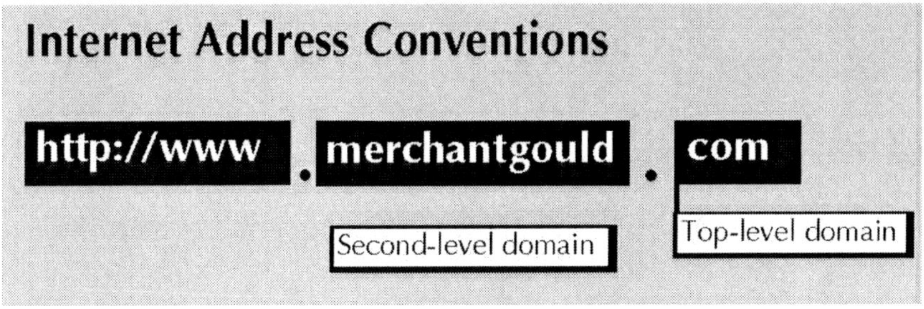

HOW TO ACQUIRE A DOMAIN NAME

Virtually anyone can register a domain name by selecting a domain name, contacting a "registrar," and paying a fee, which generally ranges from $5 to $35. The term "registrar" is used to denote an organization that is able to register an available domain name. A registrar is distinguishable from a "registry," which is a database of domain names that have been registered. Historically, Network Solutions, Inc. ("NSI") was the only registrar of domain names and was responsible for maintaining the registry for all "com," "net," and "org" Internet registrations. Today, other companies offer registrar services as well. The addition of multiple registrars is an effort to make the domain name registration process competitive. A list of all registrars accredited to register universally recognized domain names is available within the ICANN website, at http://www.icann.org/registrars/accredited-list.html. This site also provides links to websites of each individual registrar. VeriSign Global Registry Services, formerly part of NSI, now maintains the registry of "com," "net," and "org" registrations, while the rest of the top level domain registries are maintained by other organizations. A list of registry operators for other top level domains is available at http://www.iana.org/gtld/gtld.htm.

Traditionally, NSI allowed registration of domain names on a "first come, first serve" basis. By registering a domain name, registrars generally do not determine the legality of the domain name registration or otherwise evaluate whether that registration or use may infringe upon the rights of any third parties, a policy that has led to problems, particularly with respect to the rights of trademark holders.

The advent of new top level domains and their corresponding registries has raised additional problems, including (1) how initial allocation should be accomplished, and (2) how to protect the rights of current intellectual property owners without stifling freedom of expression in the free market. In response to these issues, the new registries have taken a variety of pre-registration procedures. For example, .biz registry operator Neulevel.com used a pure lottery system, whereas Afilias had a round robin system for early registrants. Some of the new registries have taken steps to provide limited protection for holders of trademark or trade name rights. For example, .biz registry operator Neulevel.com provided an IP claims service for trademark owners, and also requires that registrants agree to use the name only for "bona fide business or commercial use." For more details, see http://www.neulevel. com/ and its related links. Similarly, "info" registry operator Afilias offered a sunrise period in which owners of registered trademarks had an opportunity to pre-register their marks as domain names. For information on Afilias and the "info" top level domain, see http://www.afilias.com. The United States country code, ".US" is available and may be purchased by private entities. To qualify for a .US domain name, the registrant must have a sufficient nexus with the United States. To show a sufficient nexus, the registrant must be a U.S. citizen or resident, a U.S. business or organization, or a U.S. federal, state, or local government. Businesses with a bona fide presence in the United States can also register a .US domain name. .US domain name registrations are available through .US Accredited Registrars which can be found at http://www.nic.us/register/dotus_registrars.html. Registries for other new top level domains, such as "aero," can be found at their respective registry sites.

In order to determine if a domain name is available, NSI and other registrars offer access to the "WHOIS" database, which is available at each individual registrar's website. For example, NSI's database is accessible at http://www.networksolutions.com/whois. If no record is found for a domain name in this database, then it is available to be registered. Because the costs and requirements for registration of a domain name are minimal, it is recommended that domain names be registered prior to any final decision regarding use of the domain name, as others may register the domain name if it is available. Once a domain name is registered, it is also recommended that similar domain names be registered, if available, to prevent others from registering them. For example, the law firm Merchant & Gould has a web page located at the URL http://www.merchant gould.com. It has also registered various additional URLs, including http://www.merchant-gould.com.

Domain names are generally chosen to represent either the name of the business, or the product or service sold by the business. The value of a domain name is often associated with its ability to function as a trademark identifying the goods and services with a specific source. Prior to registering a domain name, it is recommended that a search be performed to determine whether others have a trademark registration in the domain name itself, or in words contained within the domain name. A search opinion regarding a domain name may be obtained by trademark counsel, or a quick preliminary search may be performed on the United States Patent and Trademark Office's Internet search system, at http://www.uspto.gov. As described below, the existence of a federal trademark registration for a mark identical to that of a domain name may prevent the domain name registrant from using the domain name.

DOMAIN NAME DISPUTES

Trademarks arise from using words, logos, and the like in connection with selling goods and services. As discussed above, most registrars award domain names on a first come, first served basis and do not undertake a complete trademark search for each proposed registration. Consequently, significant legal issues involving trademark or trade name conflicts can arise from registration of a domain name.

Similar, even identical, word marks can be simultaneously registered as trademarks by unrelated businesses on unrelated goods. For example, "Delta" is a trademark for airline services, water faucets, and other businesses. The problem of overlap is increased when non-registered marks are considered, since identical unregistered marks can be used in distinct geographical regions of the country for decades, even on the same goods and services, without any problems arising. Also, logo designs can distinguish marks whose words alone are similar or identical. Trade names, which are outside the scope of federal registration but may be registered as corporate names on a state-by-state basis, are another source of overlap.

In contrast, only one party can register a given domain name. Thus, while Delta Airlines and Delta Faucets can coexist, only one can lay claim to the desirable delta.com domain name. This problem is particularly prevalent in the "com" domain, since anyone may register an available "com" domain name, regardless of the type of goods, services or the part of the country in which any trademark or trade name is used. Indeed, a party may register an available "com" domain name even if *no* goods or services are associated with the term. Moreover, the problem of overlap is exacerbated because domain names are often shortened versions of trademarks or trade names, including abbreviations, and initials.

The following conflicts may arise:

- Two businesses have legitimately used the same name or mark on different products or services, and both want to use it as a domain name.

- Two businesses in different parts of the country or the world have similar marks or names, and want to use the same word or phrase as a domain name.

- Two businesses with different marks or names seek similar names because one (or both) seeks to shorten its mark in a way which makes the domain name similar or identical.

- An unscrupulous competitor or third party (a "pirate") anticipates your desire for a particular domain name and obtains it first. This process of registering a domain name with the purpose of selling it to a trademark holder or simply to the highest bidder is commonly termed "cybersquatting."

In order to sort out the difficulties that arise from the conflict between the first come, first served registration system for domain names and the multiple user structure of trademark law, ICANN has enacted a dispute resolution policy that applies to all domain names. You can review this policy at http://www.icann.org/udrp/udrp-policy-24oct99.htm. These guidelines, which become part of the agreement entered into upon registration of a domain name, indicate that it is the domain name registrant (as opposed to the registrar or registry) who has legal responsibility to determine whether a given domain name infringes someone else's rights. The domain name registrant indemnifies registrars against any such liability.

ICANN Domain Name Dispute Policy

Prior to the enactment of ICANN's dispute resolution policy (commonly known as the "UDRP"), NSI had enacted a dispute resolution system that permitted a trademark owner to challenge a registration where the domain name was identical to the registered trademark, and was registered after the registration date of the trademark. If these factors were met, NSI would put the registration on hold. In part due to public dissatisfaction with the NSI policy, ICANN took over domain name dispute resolutions under a series of agreements approved by the United States government.

There is currently serious consideration regarding restructuring the ICANN domain name dispute policy. The current ICANN domain name dispute policy:

- requires that the cybersquatter registered and used the domain name in "bad faith" and lacks any "right or legitimate interest" in the name;
- is no longer limited to federal mark owners and can be now be used against holders of confusingly similar names (instead of merely identical names);
- requires the domain owner to submit to a mandatory administrative proceeding once initiated by a mark owner

with remedies limited to cancellation of the domain registration or its transfer to the mark owner;

- the entire administrative proceeding is concluded based upon the complaint and the response to the complaint (and possibly a reply) and supporting documents;
- the domain name owner has twenty (20) days in which to respond with argument to a filed complaint;
- jurisdiction for appeals of the administrative proceeding is at either the domain name holder's registered address or the jurisdiction of the registrar. In this regard, business owners may want to verify that their registrar is located in a convenient jurisdiction.

The mark holder bears the burden of proving all three of the following:

- the domain name is identical to, or confusingly similar to, a trademark;
- the domain holder has no rights or legitimate interests with respect to the domain name; and
- the domain name has been registered and is being used in bad faith.

Under the ICANN dispute policy, factors for determining bad faith include:

- acquisition of the domain name primarily for the purpose of selling, renting, or otherwise transferring the domain name registration to the owner of the trademark or to a competitor, for more than the documented costs directly related to the domain name;
- a pattern of registering for the purpose of blocking the mark owners from using names;

- registration primarily for the purpose of disrupting the business of a competitor; and

- use for commercial gain, with intent to attract users to the domain site by creating a likelihood of confusion with the mark as to the source, sponsorship, affiliation or endorsement of goods/services.

The domain name holder may counter with evidence of good faith and a legitimate interest. A domain name holder has rights or legitimate interest in a domain name if:

- the domain name holder has made prior use in connection with a good faith offer of goods or services using the name;

- the domain name holder is commonly known by the name; or

- the domain name holder is making a legitimate noncommercial or fair use of the domain name (for noncommercial gain).

Domain name holders are prevented from transferring the domain registration to another while the dispute or court proceeding regarding the domain name is pending.

The domain name holder has twenty days from the date the complaint is forwarded by the domain name service provider in order to submit a response, if any, to the provider. If the mark holder has designated a single-member panel, the domain name holder may opt for a three-member panel (and pay half of the costs). Although it is advisable to file a response, a domain name holder can prevail without doing so if the panel determines, based upon the complainant's filings alone, that the complaint is without merit.

The panel has very broad powers on the manner in which the proceeding shall be handled (generally there are no in-person hearings). In the event of any legal proceedings initiated prior to or during an administrative proceeding in respect of a domain name dispute, the panel has the discretion to decide whether to suspend or terminate the administrative proceeding, or to proceed to a decision. A domain name holder has ten (10) days to begin a court action after an adverse decision.

More information on ICANN and the UDRP is available at the ICANN website, http://www.icann.org. Links to approved dispute resolution providers are available at http://www.icann.org/udrp/approved-providers.htm.

Anticybersquatting Consumer Protection Act

On November 2, 1999, the Anticybersquatting Consumer Protection Act became law. The Act is aimed at so-called "cybersquatters" who register trademarks or names of others as domain names in order to sell them for a profit to the rightful owner. The Act provides for civil remedies without a need to prove relatedness of the goods or services of the parties. Rightful owners of trademarks or personal names may now bring an action against one who:

- has a bad-faith intent to profit from the goodwill of the trademark or personal name of another; and
- registers or uses a domain name that was identical to, confusingly similar to, or dilutive (for famous marks only) of such a mark at the time that the domain name was registered.

The Act sets out several non-exclusive factors for determining whether a person had bad faith:

- prior, bona-fide use by the person;
- non-commercial and fair use of a mark in the site by the person;
- the person's intent to divert consumers from the mark owner's online location to another site;
- the person's offer to sell the domain name to the mark owner, without having used, or having an intent to use, it in a bona fide manner;

- the person's provision of material and misleading contact information or the intentional failure to maintain accurate contact information in the registry;
- the person's registration or acquisition of multiple domain names that are identical or similar to the trademark; and
- the extent of the trademark's fame or distinctiveness.

The Act provides that a court may order the forfeiture, cancellation or transfer of the domain name. Where personal jurisdiction (as opposed to *in rem* jurisdiction, as discussed below) is established over the defendant, a plaintiff can also recover either actual damages, or statutory damages in the amount of $1,000 to $100,000 per domain name. Finally, the Act immunizes domain name registries from monetary relief.

In a representative case, Virtual Works, Inc. v. Volkswagen of Am., Inc., 238 F.3d 264 (4th Cir. 2001), the court found dilution, trademark infringement and cyberpiracy based upon Virtual Works' use of the domain name vw.net despite the fact that this domain name represented the initials of the company. The court did note that the company did not use the VW initials as a mark.

The Act also allows for *in rem* actions against the domain names themselves rather than the domain name holder. *In rem* jurisdiction means jurisdiction over the property as opposed to jurisdiction over the person (or personal jurisdiction). Generally, one needs to have sufficient contacts with a forum state to justify personal jurisdiction. However, when *in rem* jurisdiction is available, sufficient contacts exist if the property is located within the forum state. The court in Caesars World v. Caesars Palace.Com, 112 F. Supp. 2d 502 (E.D. Va. 2000), held that *in rem* jurisdiction over the domain name itself does not violate due process. More recently, another district court has clarified that where the defendant has no other ties to the United States, *in rem* jurisdiction is only appropriate in the judicial district in which the name was registered, FleetBoston Fin. Corp. v. www.fleetbostonfinancial.com, 138 F. Supp. 2d 121 (D. Mass 2001). Because the most popular registrar is Network Solutions, Inc. (NSI), these holdings mean that if personal jurisdiction cannot be established, many domain name suits will be subject to *in rem* jurisdiction in the District Court for the Eastern District of Virginia, since NSI is located in that judicial district.

Domain Name Use Not Necessarily Trademark Infringement

In Nissan Motor Company v. Nissan Computer Corp. No. 04-869 Petition for Cert. filed (U.S. Dec. 22, 2004) Nissan requested a review of a 9th Circuit ruling that allowed a computer business to continue using the domain name Nissan.com. An individual, Mr. Uzi Nissan had used his last name for business ventures including Nissan Computer Corp. Nissan, the automobile company, sued Mr. Nissan for trademark infringement and dilution based on the use of Nissan.com. The District Court found infringement only to the extent that the website included ads for automobile related products and prohibited Nissan Computer Corp. from linking to sites that contained negative comments about the Nissan automobile company. On appeal the Court affirmed the trademark infringement claims but reversed Plaintiff's claims of dilution. In its Petition for Certiorari., Nissan Motor Company argues that the 9th Circuit ruling was wrong in its holding that use of the domain name that was a famous mark was not subject to dilution because it was a non-commercial use, and that links were somehow protected by the First Amendment, and that no infringement took place when Nissan.com diverts consumers away from the automotive company and those looking for information on Nissan automobiles. The Supreme Court, however, refused to review the appelate court decision; and Mr. Nissan can continue to use Nissan.com.

.US Domain Dispute Resolution Policy

The .US domain name has a dispute resolution policy that is similar to the United States Anticybersquatting Consumer Protection Act and the ICANN Uniform Domain Name Resolution Policy (UDRP) and can be found at http://www.nic.us/policies/docs/usdrp.pdf. To bring an administrative action, the complainant must assert that: (i) the domain name is identical or confusingly similar to a trademark or servicemark in which the complainant has rights; (ii) the domain name holder has no rights or legitimate interests in respect of the domain name; and (iii) the domain name has been registered in bad faith or is being used in bad faith.

Bad faith can be shown if: (i) circumstances indicating that the domain name was registered or acquired primarily for the purpose of selling, renting, or otherwise transferring the domain name registration to the complainant who is the owner of the trademark or service mark or to a competitor of that complainant, for valuable consideration in excess of documented out-of-pocket costs directly related to the domain name; (ii) the domain name was registered in order to prevent the owner of the trademark or service mark from reflecting the mark in a corresponding domain name; (iii) the domain name was registered primarily for the purpose of disrupting the business of a competitor; or (iv) the domain name was registered to intentionally attract, for commercial gain, Internet users to a web site or other on- line location, by creating a likelihood of confusion with the complainant's mark as to source, sponsorship, affiliation, or endorsement.

There is also a procedure for disputing a sufficient nexus with the United States of another domain name holder. Current dispute resolution providers include the National Arbitration Forum and the American Arbitration Association.

REFERRING TO OTHER WEB SITES AND TRADEMARKS

When litigation or arbitration under the domain name dispute policy is impossible or impractical, other solutions exist to resolve disputes. Where both parties desire to use the identical domain name, cross-links may be used whereby each page provides links to the other party's page. For example, the respective owners of the "Scrabble" mark in North America and the rest of the world have found a way to share "scrabble.com" by providing a map of the world at "scrabble.com" with a link to the appropriate site associated with a geographic location. Similarly, providing links to related sites may be an acceptable resolution. Disclaimers may also be used to eliminate any possible confusion.

Where two users cannot peacefully coexist, a transfer of the domain name may be the only solution. Domain names may be bought and sold like any other property. Of course, the price of a particular domain name is what someone is willing to pay for it. For example, the record price for a domain name sale appears to be business.com, which was recently purchased for $7.5 million.

TRADEMARKS AND THE INTERNET

TRADEMARK LAW

A trademark or service mark is a word, name, symbol or device used to identify goods or services and distinguish them from others. Trademarks and service marks indicate both the source of origin and quality of the goods or services with which they are associated.

The selection of a trademark may be very important in terms of the trademark owner's ability to obtain federal registration and prevent others from using the mark. For those businesses intending to offer goods or services over the Internet, the selection of a trademark should be done in connection with registering the domain name. Typically, legal counsel is consulted regarding whether federal registration of the mark is likely in view of the inherent qualities of the mark (i.e., whether it is generic, descriptive, suggestive, or arbitrary) and based upon the use of similar or identical marks by others. A quick WHOIS search at NSI's web site at http://www.networksolutions.com/whois will identify whether the domain name has already been registered. As thousands of domain names are being registered daily, it is often a good idea to register the proposed mark as a domain name early in order to insure its availability.

Although federal registration of a mark is not necessary to use the mark, registration does provide substantial procedural advantages if the trademark owner should ever be faced with the task of stopping a potential infringer. Furthermore, a federal trademark registration for a mark identical to a domain name may have tremendous value when involved in a domain name dispute under either the ACPA or the UDRP, as discussed in the preceding section.

Once a trademark has been federally registered, it should be identified either with the word "registered" or with the symbol ®. An unregistered trademark should be identified with the letters (tm) placed in close association with the word™ or symbol that is the trademark.

A domain name in and of itself is not necessarily a trademark, although many domain names attain trademark status because they are used to identify the source of particular goods or services. Similarly, registration of a domain name alone does not create priority for later trademark rights in a domain name, even if the domain name was registered before the trademark's registration, Brookfield Communications. v. West Coast Entertainment, 174 F.3d 1036 (9th Cir. 1999). In *Brookfield*, the court held that priority would be based upon the time when a party announced their web site in a public and widespread manner or otherwise attempted to create an association in the minds of consumers between the domain name and its owner. In so holding, the *Brookfield* court clarified that ownership of an intent-to-use website, without further action, does not give rise to trademark rights. Proposed marks used *only* as a domain name must be registered for the proper services. The Patent and Trademark Office (PTO) has published a position paper on registering domain names, setting forth its current policy on this issue. That paper is available at http://www.uspto.gov/web/ offices/tac/domain.

TRADEMARK INFRINGEMENT AND DILUTION

Trademark infringement occurs when one trademark is confusingly similar to another's trademark. Generally, the first to use a trademark may continue using the mark. However, the first user may be precluded from expanding the geographic region in which the mark is used if a federal registration is not obtained. Whether two trademarks are confusingly similar depends on a number of factors, including:

- The existence of actual confusion in the marketplace between the trademarks;
- Similarity of the appearance, sound and meaning of the trademarks;
- The degree of similarity between the goods and services being identified by the trademarks;
- The degree of secondary meaning acquired by the trademarks;
- The sophistication of the consumers who buy the particular products or services;
- The similarity of the channels of distribution of the products or services (that is, are they both sold in the same type of stores). Note that this factor often suggests a likelihood of confusion where both products or services are offered via the Internet;
- The degree of commercial competition between the two trademark users, and
- The distinctiveness of the trademarks.

A trademark that is "famous" may be protected against dilution from other marks or uses of the mark even if the use is on unrelated goods as long as the trademark holder can prove that the mark is being blurred or tarnished.

TOOLS FOR THE WEB

Advertising On The Internet

As a general rule, the test of legality for advertising on the Internet is similar to the test for advertising in general. Advertising must not be "false, deceptive or misleading" to the consumer. Generally, advertising may refer to other trademarks if it is not likely to cause confusion, if it is literally true, and if it is not implicitly misleading.

Use of the trademark of a competitor or another company can result in trademark infringement. Nonetheless, one can make fair use of a mark, such as through comparative advertising and through free speech to talk about another's product. To increase the likelihood such fair use will be considered permissible, care must be taken to (1) dispel any implicit affiliation with the famous mark, such as with a disclaimer; (2) use the trademark truthfully; (3) only use the trademark as much and as minimally necessary and (4) not use color schemes, logos, or other distinctive features of the competitor that are unnecessary to convey the truthful information. The fair use of the mark of another is generally a very fact specific inquiry and any factors that suggest improper motives or bad faith of some actions can result in negative implications for even legitimate other actions. When referring to another's trademark or advertising materials, a business must make sure that it does not infringe any intellectual property, including copyrights, owned by the other party. Finally, disclaimers may be advisable when referring to another's trademark.

Comparison shopping applications, which search vendor websites and produce information about lower priced options, are another new and relatively controversial method of web advertising. With regard to these and other types of web advertising, the advice of counsel may be useful to businesses in order to evaluate the potential risks involved.

The Federal Trade Commission released its staff paper "Dot Com Disclosures" in May, 2000 to guide parties using the Internet for advertising as to the applicability of product and business specific FTC laws to Internet advertising. The paper is available at http://www.ftc.gov/bcp/conline/pubs/buspubs/dotcom/index.html.

Search Engines, Banner Ads and Sponsored Links

Search engines offer advertising services to others. One service offered by many search engines is targeted advertising when a search term is entered into the search engine. A new, targeted method of advertising is to trigger the advertising based upon a computer user entering a competitor's mark into a search engine. There are at least three ways search engines appear to sell this service. First, certain search terms may result in banner ads appearing on the search result screen. Second, sponsored advertisers may appear separate from the search results. Finally, the search results may be modified to allow sponsored advertisers to appear high in the search results screen.

Although showing a banner advertisement in response to a search engine query may be akin to placing a billboard that advertised a competitive store above or next to a store and was initially considered allowable, Playboy Enterprises, Inc. v. Netscape Communications Corp, 52 USPQ2d 1162 (D.C.D.Cal. 1999), on appeal, the Northern Circuit has held that this practice may be an infringement of the trademark owner's rights. Playboy Enterprises, Inc. v. Netscape Communications, Inc., 354 F.3d 1020 (9th Cir. 2004). However, it is improper to use a competitor's trademark or other famous trademarks not owned by the company as metatags in order to trade off the good will associated with them. Brookfield Communications. v. West Coast Entertainment, 174 F.3d 1036 (9th Cir. 1999). In *Brookfield*, the Court specifically found that using another's mark as a metatag is somewhat like posting a billboard with another's trademark directing traffic to one's store and found this "initial interest" confusion actionable.

Recently litigated disputes regarding the use of another company's trademark to trigger sponsored links should also be considered. In Government Employees Ins. Co. v. Google, Inc., 2005 U.S. Dist. LEXIS 18642 (E.D. Va. Aug. 8, 2005), the court denied Google's motion to dismiss trademark infringement claims based on the use of sponsored links. While that case was eventually settled, the decision shows the use of a keyword to trigger an ad may create liability.

Other cases allege that third party pop-up advertisements that obscure the advertisements of the web page being viewed violate the trademark rights of others. For example, Gator Corp., a pop-up advertiser, has been charged by various newspapers with trademark infringement for its pop-up ad service which is associated with various news web pages. Seven publishers, including the Washington Post, New York Times, and Dow Jones, reached a settlement agreement with Gator Corps after a federal judge ordered Gator to stop displaying pop-up advertising on the publisher's web pages without permission on the grounds that the advertisements infringed their copyrights, trademarks and stole revenue from potential ads. In another case, the Court found that a pop-up advertising scheme did not support a claim of trademark infringement, unfair competition, trademark dilution, or copyright infringement. U-Haul v. WhenU.com, Inc., 279 F. Supp.2d 723 (E.D. Va. 2003)

When can one use a competitor's mark in search engines? There are no hard and fast rules in this area. The relevant claims, primarily for trademark infringement and dilution, are fact intensive. Unaffiliated websites should ideally be distinctly presented to the user as unaffiliated with the trademark owner. One should try to separate one's trademark from the actual search engine results. In this regard, it is likely better to appear as a banner ad appearing on the search result screen or as a sponsored advertiser separate from the search results than modifying the search results so that the your web page appears in the search results or higher up in the search results. The domain name should not itself create confusion, as it is typically listed in the results. Any description that appears in the search results should also avoid language suggesting affiliation or sponsorship by the trademark owner. Content found at the website should also be truthful, unlikely to exacerbate confusion, and devoid of misappropriated photographs or images. And again, the general rules of using a competitor's mark discussed above should also be followed.

Metatags

The metatag is a powerful browser tool for Internet advertising. The keyword portion of a metatag consists of hidden words that can be used to describe the contents of a web page. The metatags of a particular web site can be viewed by selecting the "view page source" or equivalent command in the web browser. The metatag is invisible to the website visitor, but is detectable by search engines, and is often used in the formula which determines search results for a particular inquiry.

Using competitors' trademarks or other famous trademarks not owned by the company as metatags, to trade off the good will associated with them, is improper. As the Ninth Circuit held in Brookfield Communications. v. West Coast Entertainment, 174 F.3d 1036 (9th Cir. 1999), using another's mark as a metatag is somewhat like posting a billboard with another's trademark directing traffic to one's store, and is therefore actionable under the initial interest confusion doctrine. Cf. Bahari v. Gross, 119 F. Supp. 2d 309 (S.D.N.Y. 2000) (recognizing the Brookfield holding, but finding fair use and lack of confusion, and refusing to grant a preliminary injunction against metatag use).

As the *Bahari* case demonstrates, where confusion is unlikely or the metatag is used to accurately convey truthful information, use of the metatag and/or a famous trademark belonging to another may be permissible. To increase the likelihood such actions will be considered permissible, care must be taken to (1) dispel any implicit affiliation with the famous mark, such as with a disclaimer; (2) use the trademark truthfully; and (3) not use color schemes, logos, or other distinctive features of the competitor that are unnecessary to convey the truthful information, Playboy Enterprises, Inc. v. Terri Welles, 7 F. Supp. 2d 1098 (S.D. Cal. 1998), aff'd, 162 F.3d 1169 (9th Cir. 1998).

Metatags may also be used in connection with advertising banners. For example, certain key words typed into search engines may direct particular advertising banners to appear. However, it is improper to have one company's advertising appear in response to a competitor's name or trademark as the keyword. Similar issues apply when using another's personal name or individually recognizable term as a metatag. The aforementioned metatag precautions apply in these situations as well.

ADVERTISING AND CHILDREN

When advertising to children, especially children under 13,

particular care should be taken. It is recommended that anyone advertising to children follow the Better Business Bureau's Children's Advertising Review Unit's ("CARU") rules and guidelines.

The CARU guidelines provide, in small part, that advertisers need to examine the total advertising message to be certain that the net communication will not mislead or misinform children. Advertisers should avoid using extreme sales pressure in advertising presentations to children. Information that requires disclosure for legal or other reasons should be in language understandable by the child audience. Disclaimers and disclosures should be clearly worded, legible and prominent. Comparative claims should be based on real product advantages that are understandable to the child audience. These guidelines can be found at http://www.caru.org.

In Ashcroft v. ACLU, 535 U.S. 564 (2004); 124 S.Ct. 2783 (2004) the United States Supreme Court decided on March 2, 2004 to bar enforcement of the Child Online Protection Act otherwise known as COPA. COPA was enacted by Congress in 1998 to protect minors from exposure to sexually explicit materials on the Internet. In a 5 to 4 vote the Supreme Court agreed with a lower court's decision that it was correct to block the law from taking effect because it was unconstitutional and violated the first amendment. The Court determined that filtering software or other technological solutions might be a superior alternative to content based restrictions of free speech. In earlier rulings COPA had been rejected based on the law not being narrowly tailored to punish commercial pornographers but instead prohibited a wide range of protected expression. The opposition to COPA has been led by the American Civil Liberties Union and supported by a wide range of other groups including the Association of American Publishers, The American Society of Newspaper Editors, the Recording Industry Association of America and others. While it has never been enforced COPA requires commercial website operators to use credit cards or other adult access systems to prevent minors from viewing their material. Notice provisions and warnings have been the common response by websites to comply with COPA. Criminal and civil penalties of up to $50,000 per day for any violations were available. It is not clear if the government will continue in its efforts to argue for enforcement of COPA or similar laws or if less restrictive legislation may be proposed.

PATENTS AND THE INTERNET

INTRODUCTION

The global proliferation of networked computers on the Internet has spawned explosive growth in patents in the United States and worldwide. The advent of the World Wide Web, e-commerce, and their associated technological advances has resulted in a multitude of innovative ideas worthy of the title "invention." Historically, great technological strides are made from a flurry of inventive activities that use or improve upon a core technological advance. The Internet clearly qualifies as such a core technological advance.

On-line entrepreneurs should consider the benefits of obtaining patent protection for unique functional features associated with their on-line businesses. While products developed for Internet commerce may be patentable, other aspects of the business may also be afforded patent protection, such as innovative features of the networking technologies and software driving the on-line business. Operators of on-line businesses must also be wary of the potential impact of infringing existing patents, in order to preemptively dodge unwelcome legal battles. The Internet itself also serves as a valuable search tool for assisting in these patent-related matters. As discussed in detail below, software and other products may be entitled to patent protection if the invention is (1) new, (2) useful, and (3) non-obvious.

PATENT SYSTEM OVERVIEW

A patent is a government grant to an inventor of the right to exclude others from making, using, selling, offering to sell, or importing an invention for a limited period of time. The government awards such monopolistic rights in exchange for the public disclosure of the invention through the patent document. Inventors are thereby rewarded for their efforts, and society benefits through the increased amount of technological knowledge made available to the public.

In order to fulfill their part of the bargain under United States patent law, inventors must disclose the best known manner for making and using the invention. The description of the invention must be sufficiently detailed to enable a person skilled in the particular technological field to make and use the invention without undue experimentation. If the invention proves to be sufficiently novel and non-obvious over existing technology, the government will in return grant the inventor a patent.

There are two types of patents that affect the Internet: utility patents and design patents. The enforceable term of a patent depends on which type of patent is obtained. A "utility patent" is available for a process, machine, manufactured article, composition, or any new and useful improvement. This type of patent covers the concept or idea behind the process, machine, composition, etc. Generally, a utility patent is enforceable for 20 years after the date on which the corresponding patent application is filed with the United States Patent and Trademark Office (USPTO). A "design patent" is available for anyone who develops an original ornamental design for a useful article of manufacture. Design patents cover the specific appearance, such as the article's shape, rather than the concept or function of the article itself. A design patent is afforded a 14-year term from its date of issuance.

STATUTORY DEADLINES

Generally, a patent application filed in the United States must be filed in the USPTO within one year of the date on which the invention is first sold, offered for sale, used publicly, or publicly disclosed such as in a printed publication. This one-year period is often referred to as a "grace period" in the United States. Failure to file the patent application within this grace period will prevent an inventor from ever obtaining patent protection for that invention. Further, it is important to note that most foreign countries do not recognize such a grace period, and those seeking foreign patent protection must file a patent application in the country in which patent protection is desired before any public disclosure or public use anywhere in the world. By way of treaties, many foreign countries do not require a patent application to be on file in that country prior to a public disclosure or use if, and only if, a patent application is already on file in a country that is a party to the treaty.

GENERAL PATENTABILITY REQUIREMENTS

Title 35 of the United States Code (35 U.S.C.) provides the federal law governing patents as enacted by Congress pursuant to a Constitutional grant of authority. 35 U.S.C. §101 sets forth patentable categories of subject matter, consisting of processes, machines, articles of manufacture, compositions of matter, or any new and useful improvement of the same. Generally, a "process" refers to a method, operation, step or series of steps performed upon some subject matter leading to a useful, concrete and tangible result. A process performed on a computer to provide a useful result would therefore be patentable subject matter. A "machine" includes mechanisms, mechanical devices and combinations that perform some function and produce a certain effect or result. "Compositions of matter" often arise in the chemical or biotechnical arena, and include physical mixtures of two or more ingredients. A "manufacture," or "article of manufacture," is a comprehensive catch-all category providing a residual class of "product" patents. Improvements to existing machines, processes, manufactures or compositions of matter also constitute patentable subject matter.

In addition to being among one of the statutory classes, an invention must prove to be new, useful and non-obvious compared to known technology and subject matter. 35 U.S.C. §101-103 sets forth these statutory requirements.

For an invention to be "new" under 35 U.S.C. §102, the invention must not have been known or used by others in the United States before the date of the patent applicant's invention. Further, the invention must not have been patented or described in a printed publication anywhere in the world, or in public use or on sale in the United States, more than one year prior to the application filing date in the United States.

The obviousness requirement is set forth in 35 U.S.C. §103, and proves to be the most troublesome requirement to satisfy. Even an invention that is considered "new" under §102 must also prove to be non-obvious over subject matter already known or available to the public. If arriving at the inventive subject matter would have been "obvious" to a hypothetical person of ordinary skill in that technological field who has access to all the currently-available information in that field, a patent may not be obtained.

PATENT APPLICATION PROCESS

Even prior to the application process with the USPTO, a potential patent applicant should consider conducting a search of the prior art to help determine the likelihood of ultimately obtaining patent protection for an invention. A rudimentary search may include an on-line search for existing patents, publications, or other prior art. Discovering prior art directed to the invention may preclude the applicant's ability to obtain patent protection. Patent practitioners can assist in conducting patent searches, and can provide an opinion as to the likelihood of the invention's patentability. If it appears that the invention is novel and non-obvious over the prior art, a patent application must be prepared and filed to obtain patent protection.

A patent application includes a written description of the invention, drawings, and claims that define the invention. The description and drawings of the invention must adequately articulate the invention such that a person skilled in that technical area could make and use the invention without undue experimentation. When complete, the patent application is submitted to the USPTO. Unless special circumstances apply, patent examiners review patent applications in their field of expertise in the order that they are received. It can often take up to a year or more from the time the application is filed to the time of first examination by the USPTO.

PATENT RESEARCH ON THE INTERNET

As is true for Internet research in general, the Internet is becoming an increasingly valuable tool for locating patent-related information. There are numerous reasons why a business owner may want to research patent information. A general understanding of United States or foreign patent laws may be desired, or actual patents or technical information may be sought out to determine whether an invention is potentially patentable, or potentially infringes another's patent. Patent searching may also be conducted to find patents or other published material that may potentially invalidate another's patent, such as a competitor, and may also be used to assess the proprietary positions of other companies.

Likewise, companies that may potentially have inventive ideas should consider placing restrictions on how information relating to the ideas is disseminated. Information that is randomly placed on company web sites without purging innovative ideas runs the risk that the information may later be used to invalidate a patent relating to the ideas. Courts have expanded the idea of what constitutes "prior art" to include information that is retrieved from the Internet. Prior art includes publications, patents or devices that were publicly known before filing of the patent application. In order to ensure that protection for inventions is not jeopardized, businesses must be careful when placing information online.

One popular Internet site for patent information is the USPTO web site, which can be found at www.uspto.gov. The U.S. Government provides free access to the United States patent database, which includes full text and images of U.S. patents issued since January 1, 1976. Access to the World Intellectual Property Organization (WIPO) PCT Patent Gazette is also provided, which allows searching of foreign patent applications filed in accordance with the Patent Cooperation Treaty. The USPTO web site also provides a wide variety of other information related to the patenting process.

PATENT INFRINGEMENT

A patentee obtains the right to exclude others from making, using, offering for sale, or selling the invention throughout the United States, or importing the invention into the United States. If the invention is a process, the patentee obtains the right to exclude others from using, offering for sale, or selling throughout the United States or importing into the United States products made by that process.

On-line sellers of products could potentially be liable for patent infringement. Patents related to electronic transactions using the Internet are being granted by the USPTO. For example, the E-Data Corporation owns a patent that covers electronic point-of-sale transactions involving digital data. The patent is related to manufacturing and distributing information embodying material objects by using point of sale machines that are in communication with a common host. Since the inventor of this process is Charles C. Freeny, Jr., it has become known as the "Freeny Patent." Several thousand companies involved in electronic commerce have been contacted by E-Data and been asked to pay royalties. Some of these companies even entered into licensing agreements, including IBM and Adobe Systems.

It is not clear to what extent the Freeny Patent covers electronic commerce or if it will have only limited application. However, case law has begun to to define its scope. In Interactive Gift Express, Inc. v. CompuServe, Inc., 47 U.S.P.Q.2d 1797 (S.D.N.Y. 1998), the plaintiff alleged that CompuServe contributorily infringed and induced infringement by offering computer software via the Internet. The court suggested a very limited scope of the Freeny Patent and concluded that it applied only to electronic purchases made by buyers using kiosk-type terminal equipment in a retail setting and not any place where a computer was located and used to reproduce information in a material object for a price. However, the Federal Circuit vacated and remanded the decision, holding that the lower court erred on the construction of the claim limitations and interpreted the patent too narrowly, Interactive Gift Express, Inc. v. CompuServe, Inc., 2001 U.S.App. LEXIS 15711 (Fed. Cir. July 13, 2001).

Patent rights associated with the basic process of electronic transactions will certainly have a significant impact on the development of electronic commerce using the Internet. High speed modems, which are critical to the commercial future of the Internet, have also been the subject of patent claims and conflicts. It will be interesting to monitor the extent to which patents are actually issued by the USPTO for Internet related technology and whether such patents will impede or bolster the expansion of electronic commerce on the Internet. The following section discusses the wide range of Internet related inventions that may be patentable.

United States Patent [19] | **[11] Patent Number: 4,528,643**

Freeny, Jr. | **[45] Date of Patent: Jul. 9, 1985**

---

[54] **SYSTEM FOR REPRODUCING INFORMATION IN MATERIAL OBJECTS AT A POINT OF SALE LOCATION**

[75] Inventor: **Charles C. Freeny, Jr.,** Fort Worth, Texas

[73] Assignee: **FPDC, Inc.,** Oklahoma City, Okla.

[21] Appl. No. **456,730**

[22] Filed **Jan. 10, 1983**

[31] **Int. Cl G06F 1/00**

[52] **U.S. CL 364/900**

[58] **Field of Search** ....364/200 MS File, 900 MS File

[56] **References Cited**

U.S. PATENT DOCUMENTS

3,829.813	9/1974	FREENY, JR.,	
3,911,397	10/1975	FREENY, JR.,	
3,924,065	12/1976	FREENY, JR.,	
3,945,220	3/1976	Brobeck et al.,	
1,970,952	7/1976	Boohrogrd et al.,	
4,071,911	1/1978	Mazur	364/900
4,112,433	9/1978	Freeny, Jr.	
4,209,787	1/1980	Freeny, Jr.	
4,217,588	8/1980	Freeny, Jr.	
4,220,991	9/1980	Ramane et al.	
4,232,317	11/1980	Freeny, Jr.	
4,265,371	5/1981	Desei et. al.	
4,270,182	5/1981	Asija	
4,228,544	5/1982	Maidwin et. al.	

Primary Examiner–Raulie H. Zache
Attorney, Agent, or Firm–Dunlap & Codding

[27] **ABSTRACT**

The present invention contemplates a system for reproducing information in material objects at a point of sale location wherein the information to be reproduced is provided at the point of sale location from a location remote with respect to the point of sale location, an owner authorization code is provided to the point of sale location in response to receiving a request code from the point of sale location requesting to reproducing predetermined information in a material object, and the predetermined information is reproduced in a material object at the point of sale location in response to receiving the owner authorization code.

56 Claims, 4 Drawing Figures

PATENTING INTERNET-RELATED SUBJECT MATTER

While it is perhaps easy to comprehend the patentability of a machine, manufacture or other piece of "hardware," it is not as readily apparent for other less "tangible" inventions, such as software and related computer processes.

Software, computer processes, and graphical user interfaces are but a few examples of on-line technology available for patent protection. A utility patent can protect inventive functions, methods, systems or algorithms, including applied mathematical formulas, which are used or embodied in a software product. The following provides some guidance on the types of subject matter that on-line business owners and operators should recognize as potentially patentable. As software is the main patentable subject matter for Internet transactions, this discussion will focus on software. However, similar principles apply to other patentable subject matter.

First, entrepreneurs may want to sell a product by way of the Internet. Where the business is merely acting as a retail distribution center, any intellectual property rights in the product vest with the designer of the product, not the business owner. However, many businesses develop their own products to be sold via traditional and electronic commerce channels. In these cases, business owners should consider whether the product or products themselves are worthy of patent protection.

Potential patent protection related to the on-line business does not end there, however. Even where the product(s) being sold is not the creation of the business owner, patentable subject matter may lie in the manner in which the business avails itself to the electronic purchasers. For example, a unique software program or application developed to facilitate purchasing products from the on-line store can be patentable in and of itself. A program created to more quickly and efficiently display or order products could be successfully patented if novel and non-obvious over presently-existing software applications. Further, the purpose of the on-line store may be to sell a service, rather than a deliverable product. A good example of such a service is software used to make financial transactions or stock trades. No product is actually delivered, but a service is provided for a cost. In these cases, business owners may market their service as being better than the competition. What makes the service "better" could potentially be a patentable invention, and an issued patent could give the patent owner a competitive edge.

Business owners may proclaim that they are software-illiterate, and are incapable of inventing sophisticated, patentable software. Even if this is true, it does not prevent the proprietor from "owning" the patent rights. If development of such software requires the business owner to seek professional services from a software company or individual programmer, the patent rights can be retained by requiring, via contract, that the program's creator assign all patent rights to the business owner.

Utility Patents

Many inventions related to the Internet have been patented. Patents relating to electrical communication, data storage and retrieval, cryptography, information processing, and system organization are a few of the many Internet-related patents. A large portion of patent issues associated with the Internet are those surrounding software patents. Traditionally, software has been protected under copyright law. However, computer software may also be granted patent protection. Given a choice between copyright and patent protection, software developers generally prefer patent protection, as it provides greater protection than copyright. To obtain patent protection, the software must do more than solve a mathematical problem, as algorithms and abstract ideas are considered laws of nature and are therefore not patentable. For a discussion of copyrightability of software, see the Copyrightable Subject Matter discussion in the Copyright Law section.

Various types of functional software applications can be protected by utility patents, including word processing applications, compilers, web browsers, database programs, spreadsheets, utility programs, language translation programs, and even computer games. Utility patents can also protect aspects of the software design other than the main functional application, such as control functions, editing functions and data structures. Data transmission schemes are also commonly the subject of utility patents, including communications protocols, encryption and data compression techniques.

Software that uses a mathematical algorithm or abstract idea may be protected by a utility patent if the inventor imposes sufficient limitations on the invention as to avoid preemption of the claimed algorithm or idea. The USPTO has identified several "safe harbors" where an invention can be patented if it: (1) incorporates sufficient "post-solution" activity; (2) incorporates sufficient "pre-solution" activity; or (3) is sufficiently limited to a practical application. Sufficient post-solution activity exists if the invention performs physical operations after using the mathematical algorithm. Merely conveying the result of a calculation, however, is not sufficient. Sufficient pre-solution activity exists if the data used in the mathematical algorithm represents measurements of physical objects or activities outside the computer. A mere data gathering step, however, is not sufficient. The measurements must be transformed into data before being used in the mathematical algorithm. Sufficient limitation to a practical application exists only when specified in the claim language.

In State Street Bank & Trust v. Signature Financial Group, 149 F.3d 1368 (Fed. Cir. 1998), *cert. denied*, 525 U.S. 1093 (1999), the Federal Circuit held that a processing system that takes data representing discrete dollar amounts through a series of mathematical calculations to determine a share price was patentable subject matter because the final result was a useful, concrete, and tangible result. The computer system, identified by Signature Financial Group as Hub and Spoke®, facilitates a structure whereby mutual funds (Spokes) pool their assets in an investment portfolio (Hub) organized as a partnership. The Court noted that a process facilitated by a computing arrangement is a "machine," or in some cases a "process," either of which is statutorily available for patent protection. In sum, the Court's ruling reveals that nearly any software-related invention producing a useful, concrete and tangible result is patentable subject matter.

Business Method Patents

Business method patents are utility patents that claim processes related to the operation of a business, and that relate to the accuracy, yield, profitability, or performance of the business. Although the patent claims often recite software and/or a computer system, neither is required to be patentable. Courts have found that there is no statutory or policy basis for excluding a business method from statutory patentable subject matter if the claimed method is within the class of patentable subject matter (i.e., not an abstract idea) and is useful, novel, and non-obvious. These patents are important because any company that develops or acquires such a patent can stop others from using the patented business method, or charge a fee for others to use it.

Many different aspects of software may be patentable. The concept driven by the software may be entitled to patent protection. For example, in State Street, discussed above, the Federal Circuit held that a data processing system that implemented an investment structure for use as an administrator and accounting agent for mutual funds constituted patentable subject matter. The Court noted that a process facilitated by a computing arrangement is a "machine," or in some cases a "process," either of which are statutorily available for patent protection. This case confirmed that business method patents were indeed patentable subject matter.

The *State Street* case has opened the door to a large number of business method patents. Amazon.com recently obtained a U.S. patent for a "one-click" on-line sales method. The "one-click" sales method involves purchasing items over the Internet with a single click of a mouse. The prior art methods utilize a two-step process in which the item to be purchased is placed in a "shopping cart" and is then "checked out." Just over two months after issuance of its patent, Amazon.com successfully obtained a preliminary injunction against Barnesandnoble.com's "Express Lane," which used a sales method for purchasing items with a single mouse click, Amazon.com, Inc. v. Barnesandnoble.com, Inc., 53 U.S.P.Q.2d 1115

(W.D. Wash. 1999). The Federal Circuit vacated the preliminary injunction, though it agreed with the lower court that the patent had been infringed, stating that Barnesandnoble.com had mounted a substantial challenge to the validity of the patent based on prior art, Amazon.com, Inc. v. Barnesandnoble.com, Inc., 57 U.S.P.Q.2d 1747 (Fed. Cir. 2001). Although the case was vacated and remanded, the Court did not question the validity of the subject matter of the patent, indicating that the "one-click" business method is patentable subject matter.

Critics contended that that the PTO is ill-equipped to investigate if an Internet business method is novel or nonobvious. In response, the PTO added a "layer of review" to business method patent applications and hired technology specialists, particularly in the area of financial systems, to aid examiners. How this policy will affect the popular opinion of the patentability of business methods remains to be seen.

Design Patents

As mentioned above, a "design patent" is available for anyone who develops an original ornamental design for a useful article of manufacture. While utility patents protect functional aspects of technology, design patents protect the appearance of an article of manufacture or material portion of the article. The standard of novelty is whether the prior art (i.e., existing designs, knowledge, descriptions, patents or other public information), contains an article having substantially the same appearance as viewed by an ordinary observer.

For the on-line entrepreneur, design patents may be significant in order to protect their internationally advertised goods. As in the case of utility patents, a product sold via the Internet may be afforded design patent protection. For example, a manufacturer of shoes or chairs might consider obtaining a design patent for the aesthetic appearance of the article.

Perhaps more importantly for providers of e-commerce is the role of design patents for software-related ornamentation. While having a somewhat tumultuous history, it is now clear that computer-generated icons are "designs" within the meaning of the statute, but must be embodied in an article of manufacture to satisfy the statute. The Manual of Patent Examining Procedure states that the icon can be embodied in an article of manufacture by visually illustrating the icon as part of a computer screen, monitor, other display panel or a portion thereof.

While less clear, a graphical screen image or web page could also be the subject of a design patent. Copyright law has traditionally been the manner of protecting screen images, but a screen image providing an operable interface could be construed as an uncopyrightable "method of operation." Design patent protection may, therefore, be a more viable option for these types of screen images, although it would be prudent to also register them as copyrighted material. It is also important to have appropriate written agreements with employees and independent contractors to make sure that inventions and other intellectual property, including copyright, belongs to the company and not the individual or outside vendor. See Work-Made-For-Hire discussion in the Copyright Law section.

TRADE SECRET PROTECTION VERSUS PATENT PROTECTION

Generally, a trade secret is information such as a formula, pattern, compilation, compound, device, mechanism, method, or technique that provides some actual or potential value to its owner, is not known to or discovered by others, and is maintained in secrecy by its owner. As long as all trade secret requirements are maintained, trade secret protection will persist, i.e., there is no expiration of trade secrets based on duration of ownership.

State law governs trade secrets, and therefore varies from state to state. An important common thread, however, is the necessity to maintain the information in secrecy. Legal remedies for misappropriation of a trade secret are surrendered upon breach of this secrecy, on the grounds that the information has consequently fallen into the public domain and is no longer a secret. It is this characteristic of trade secret law that is at odds with patent law policy, thereby sharply dividing these two forms of intellectual property protection.

Specific information or subject matter is therefore incapable of being protected by both trade secrets and patents, as these forms of protection are mutually exclusive. This is not to say that concurrent protection for related, yet different subject matter cannot be obtained. For example, trade secret and patent protection may be cooperatively used to patent a software process while maintaining the underlying source and object code as a trade secret. While United States patent law requires that the best mode for carrying out the invention be disclosed in a patent application, the United States Court of Appeals for the Federal Circuit has held that the actual program code need not necessarily be disclosed in order to meet this obligation. Whether program code needs to be disclosed in a patent application depends on the nature of the particular software invention, but most often does not require its disclosure, and may therefore be maintained as a trade secret.

Although protection of software is available under both patent and copyright laws, trade secret protection remains an important instrument. In some instances, trade secret protection can be the most effective form of software protection because its protection is immediate and can be perpetual in duration.

COPYRIGHT LAW

GENERALLY

Copyrightable Subject Matter

The Constitution of the United States provides Congress with the power to grant authors and inventors the exclusive right to their respective writings and discoveries as necessary to promote the progress of science and useful arts. Congress established copyright laws to provide copyright owners with a specific set of exclusive rights with regard to the material they create. Copyright ownership can be obtained in the following categories of materials (17 U.S.C. § 102(a)):

(1) Literary works;
(2) Musical works (including lyrics);
(3) Dramatic works (including music);
(4) Pantomimes/choreographic works;
(5) Pictorial, graphic, and sculptural works;
(6) Motion picture/audio visual works;
(7) Sound recordings; and
(8) Architectural works.

To the extent that any of the above works are original works of authorship fixed in a tangible medium of expression, they are entitled to protection under the copyright laws. The work must be original and creative, but not necessarily novel as is required in patent law. The work must simply be an independent creation that is not copied from any other work. See Feist Publications Inc. v. Rural Telephone Service Co., 499 U.S. 340 (1991).

A database may qualify as copyrightable subject matter. While individual facts or ideas are not copyrightable, a collection of data that is selected or arranged in a unique way may constitute a compilation and may be protected under the United States Copyright Act (17 U.S.C. § 101). According to *Feist*, a compilation must, however, contain a minimum level of creativity to be copyrightable. The database must be original in its selection, coordination, and arrangement. *Feist* rejected the "sweat of the brow" argument, which took into consideration the time and effort expended to create the database. Even uncopyrightable databases may be protected through a contract or license that limits the use of the database. See ProCD, Inc. v Zeidenberg Inc., 86 F.3d 1447 (7th Cir. 1996). While acknowledging in *ProCD* that the database at issue - a compilation of names, addresses and phone numbers - may not have been sufficiently original to be copyrightable, the defendant in *ProCD* was still held liable for breach of contract based upon the terms of the shrink-wrap license.

Computer programs have also been deemed copyrightable subject matter. Computer programs receive protection under the category of literary works. The most protectable elements of computer programs reside with the object and source codes. See Control Data Sys., Inc. v. Infoware, Inc., 903 F. Supp. 1316 (D. Minn. 1995). This is because such codes represent expressions, rather than ideas. According to Control Data, the program's main purpose and structure receive the least protection because such elements constitute abstract ideas, and ideas are never entitled to copyright protection.

Obtaining Copyright Protection

Copyright protection attaches immediately when the work is established in a fixed form. To obtain copyright protection you need not register or submit an application. There are, however, significant advantages to federal registration, which may warrant the copyright owner's pursuit and compliance with the formalities of registering their copyright with the United States Copyright Office. Registration preserves statutory damages and the right to obtain attorneys fees if you prevail in a copyright infringement action. Registration is also required prior to suing in any federal court and provides some evidence of presumed ownership.

In addition, a copyright notice is also no longer required to maintain copyright protection. There remain, however, significant advantages under United States copyright laws to include such a notice on any published work. To be effective, the copyright notice must contain three elements:

(1) The letter "c" in a circle, such as "©," the word "Copyright," or the abbreviation "Copr.";

(2) The year of first publication of the work; and

(3) The full name of the owner of the copyright.

In some countries, "All Rights Reserved" must appear and only the © is acceptable. A copyright notice might therefore appear as follows:

© Copyright 2001 XYZ, Inc. All Rights Reserved.

While it is impossible to copyright an idea, once the idea is expressed in a tangible form, the fixed tangible expression itself becomes subject to the copyright laws. Therefore, works of authorship fixed in digital storage devices are within the scope of copyright protection.

COPYRIGHTED MATERIALS ON THE INTERNET

If you transmit images via the Internet or allow for such transmission, you may also be considered a publisher of copyrighted material. As noted above, many different types of materials may be protected by copyright, including audiovisual works, musical compositions, sound recordings, visual art, photographs, graphics, animation, databases and computer programs. Such copyrightable materials are used throughout the Internet.

The creators of these original works of authorship retain the exclusive rights to: (1) make copies; (2) prepare derivative works; (3) distribute the copies of the work; (4) publicly perform literary, musical, dramatic, choreographic, pantomime, motion picture, and other audiovisual works; (5) publicly display literary, musical, dramatic, choreographic, pantomime, pictorial, graphical, sculptural, and individual images of audiovisual works; and (6) publicly perform sound recordings through digital audio transmission. These rights exist even without federal registration of the copyright. The right to prevent copying may be infringed as the Internet creates electronic access to copyrighted material, allowing reproduction of such materials to occur. For example:

- Copyrighted material may be copied into the memory of a computer;
- A printed document may be converted into a digital file;
- Photographs, motion video and sound recordings may be converted into digital form;
- A digital file may be uploaded or downloaded to a bulletin board system or other server;
- A file may be transferred from one user on a network to another;
- Browsing a document that resides on a web site may require the creation of a copy to display the information on another computer screen;
- Audio or audiovisual files may be transmitted; and
- Web sites may be cached, which creates copies of a web page and its content.

All of the above might be construed as an infringement of the exclusive right of the copyright owner to make copies of and distribute their work. On the Internet, however, where an unlimited number of copyrighted materials can be made instantaneously available to a large number of people around the world, and each of these people can interact with and manipulate that material quickly and easily, it is difficult to enforce the copyright laws. At the same time, virtually every transmission on the Internet is likely to implicate some right of copyright owners, because copies of material can be made and distributed continually without explicit permission. To protect copyrights, many web sites contain explicit statements that restrict copying and require information to be used for personal use only. (For a discussion of web site disclaimers and notices see the section entitled Contracts Web Site Disclaimers and Notices).

Website and Data Not Copyright Infringement

A Florida court found no copyright infringement when a competitor website used an Internet "spider" software program to extract and copy information from a competitor's website. The court determined that the extraction of what were deemed facts and their copying constituted fair use. Both websites allowed brokers to post listings of boats available for sale including pictures and descriptions. The Court determined that the individual brokers and not the website owner owned the copyrights in the pictures and descriptions posted on the website. The Court also rejected Plaintiff's claims that the compilation of listings, the headings used on the website, or the "look and feel" of the website were infringed by Defendant. Nautical Solutions Marketing Inc. v. Boats.com 2004 WL 73121 (M.D.FLA. April 1, 2004).

DATABASE PROTECTION

Although there have been many recent attempts to increase copyright protection for databases in the United States, Congress has yet to find a solution that would allow protection beyond the mere selection and arrangement of the work without providing the copyright owner with a monopoly in the information contained in the database. Proposed legislation such as the Database Investment and Intellectual Property Anti Piracy Act of 1996 (HR 3531) demonstrate efforts to extend protection to the creators and owners of databases that are not currently protected under United States copyright laws. *This legislation has not to date been enacted in the United States.*

Currently, databases are given greater protection in Europe. In 1996, the European Union adopted the Directive on the Legal Protection of Databases ("EU Directive"). The EU Directive basically rewards the "sweat of the brow" approach rejected by the United States Supreme Court in Feist. The EU Directive allows for protection of a database if it is sufficiently original or if its creation required a substantial investment of time and effort to compile the data. The Database Directive applies, however, only to databases created by developers whose countries provide reciprocal rights to databases developed by companies within the European Union. The United States does not have such reciprocal rights. Therefore, the EU Directive could have a significant impact on United States companies conducting business in the European Union because the U.S. companies will not be afforded the same, broader, protection for their databases.

My Web Grocer LLC v. Hometown Info Inc. 375 F.3rd 190 (2nd Cir. July 13, 2004) illustrates the difficulty in protecting databases based upon copyright solely based upon the selection and arrangement of information. The Court denied a preliminary injunction that would have prevented Defendant from using grocery product descriptions for on-line shopping that had been developed and copyrighted by Plaintiff. The Court questioned whether the product descriptions constituted copyrightable subject matter.

USE OF LICENSING

The exclusive rights held by the copyright owner can be licensed to other parties. This license provides the user with permission to use the copyrighted work without infringing the copyright. Therefore, it is essential that any on-line business that makes considerable use of another party's copyrightable subject matter determine to what extent a clearance of rights is necessary or if a license should be obtained.

When seeking a license from the copyright owner, one should make sure that the party granting the license is in fact authorized to provide the license. In Tasini v. New York Times Co., 972 F. Supp. 804 (S.D.N.Y. 1997), a group of freelance writers sued the owner of an electronic database and the producer of CD-ROM products as well as several newspaper and magazine publishing companies, alleging the electronic distribution of their articles infringed their copyrights. The freelance writers contributed articles to be included as part of a collection of works within the newspapers and magazines. The Second Circuit Court of Appeals, in Tasini v. New York Times Co., 206 F.3d 161 (2nd Cir. 1999), reversed the lower court ruling, which found that the placement of copyrighted works on databases is merely an "editorial revision" and therefore not infringing. The Second Circuit Court of Appeals reasoned that just as a publisher, who is granted the right to distribute an article as part of a collection, is not permitted to sell a hard copy of an individual article without the author's consent, the publisher is also not allowed to sell such an article through electronic means. The Supreme Court affirmed, emphasizing that while the publishers owned the copyright to the collective works, the authors retained all other rights related to their individual contributions to the collection, absent an express transfer of such rights. See New York Times Co. v. Tasini, 121 S. Ct. 2381 (2001).

When considering publication rights, it is important to consider the scope of the license. Some previously obtained license agreements may not have granted broad enough rights to cover the Internet and may even be limited to rights appropriate to motion picture and television only. If a company is currently preparing an agreement, it should make sure that the language is broad enough to cover all media and methods or technologies that are now known or will be created in the future. Content providers and publishers/distributors of content on the Internet must consider the copyright laws and how they impact specific activities. It is recommended that written agreements be entered into with any content provider, on-line network service, or other parties to the extent copyrighted material will be created or distributed via the Internet.

INTERNET SERVICE PROVIDERS

Liability Of Internet Service Providers

Internet service providers ("ISPs") provide their subscribers with on-line Internet access. This raises the question of whether the ISP or the individual subscriber is liable for potential copyright infringement.

Prior to the enactment of the Digital Millennium Copyright Act ("DCMA"), the law was unclear on the extent to which ISPs could be held liable for infringement by their subscribers. In Playboy Enterprises Inc. v. Frena, 839 F.Supp. 1552 (M.D. Fla. 1993), Playboy obtained summary judgment for copyright infringement against a bulletin board operator who allowed Playboy photographs to be uploaded, displayed, and downloaded. The Court found direct copyright infringement even though the bulletin board operator testified that he did not know, and had no reason to know, of the infringements. In Sega Entertainment, Ltd. v. Maphia, 857 F.Supp. 679 (N.D. Cal. 1994), Sega obtained a preliminary injunction against a bulletin board operator who encouraged the uploading and downloading of Sega games. The United States Copyright Act, through the enactment of the DMCA, now provides Internet service providers with some additional protections.

Safe Harbors For Internet Service Providers

The DMCA, Title II, Public Law 105-304, which is codified in 17 U.S.C. § 512 of the Copyright Act, provides safe harbors from copyright infringement liability for ISPs (including company bulletin boards and intra-company e-mail). To qualify for any of the safe harbors provided by the DMCA, an ISP must adopt, implement, and inform subscribers of a policy of termination for repeat infringers. In addition, the ISP must accommodate standard copyright protection measures. There are four categories of safe harbors provided by the DMCA: (1) transitory digital network communications; (2) system caching; (3) information residing on systems or networks at direction of users; and (4) information location tools. To receive the benefit of limited liability under any one of these safe harbors, the ISP must meet certain requirements. The safe harbors allow ISPs to avoid monetary damages, and, in most cases, injunctive relief for copyright infringement.

To be eligible for the transitory digital network communications safe harbor, an ISP cannot initiate the transmission of copyrighted material, the transmission must be carried out through an automatic technical process, the ISP must not select the recipients of the copyrighted material, and the ISP must not store the material any longer than is necessary to transmit it to the recipient. In this type of situation, the ISP is merely acting as a passive conduit for the material. See 17 U.S.C. § 512(a).

The system caching safe harbor requires that the copyrighted material is made available by someone other than the ISP, that the material pass through the ISP to another person, and that the transmission is carried out through an automatic technical process. Additionally, the ISP must not modify the transmitted material, must comply with the rules regarding refreshing and reloading set forth by whoever made the material available, and must not interfere with the technology that returns the material to whoever made the material available. The ISP can only remove or disable access to the material if the material is first removed or disabled from the originating site, or a court order has been entered requiring removal or disablement. See 17 U.S.C. § 512(b).

Information residing on systems or networks at direction of users allows the ISP to limit their liability for the storage of infringing material for subscribers on a system or network operated by the ISP. This safe harbor requires that the ISP has no actual knowledge of the infringing activity and does not receive a financial benefit from the infringing material. The ISP must also act expeditiously, once notice is received, to remove or disable any allegedly infringing material. Because of the notice requirement, an ISP must have a designated agent to receive notice on file with the Copyright Office. See 17 U.S.C. § 512(c).

One should be careful when sending out cease and desist letters to ISPs based on the DMCA. Diebold, Inc., the manufacturer of voting machines, sent out many cease and desist letters to ISPs after internal documents describing problems with the Diebold software were published on the Internet, including several college sites. After receiving a letter from Diebold, Swarthmore College required students to remove the allegedly infringing material. Diebold stopped sending cease and desist letters after being challenged in a lawsuit filed by the Online Policy Group on behalf of two Swarthmore College students. The judge, however, found that Diebold was liable for damages, since it knowingly and materially misrepresented that copyright infringement had occurred and that no reasonable copyright holder could have believed that portions of emails discussing possible technical problems with voting machines were protected by copyright. Online Policy Group v. Diebold, Inc., 337 F. Supp. 2d 1195 (September 2004).

Finally, information location tools qualify as a safe harbor. Information location tools allow ISPs to refer or link subscribers to other on-line locations, some of which may contain infringing material. The ISP must not have actual knowledge of the infringing activity and if knowledge is present must act expeditiously to remove or disable any infringing material, and must not receive a financial benefit from the infringing activity. The ISP is only required to comply with these requirements if notice of the infringement sufficiently identifies the material or activity to allow the ISP to locate the allegedly infringing material. See 17 U.S.C. § 512(d).

FAIR USE

Along with the previously discussed alternatives for avoiding or limiting liability for infringement (see discussion of licensing in the section of this Guide entitled Copyright Law, Safe Harbors for On-Line Service Providers) there is the doctrine of fair use. Fair use is a defense to copyright infringement, which is codified in 17 U.S.C. § 107 of the Copyright Act. Fair use allows copyrighted work to be used without authorization from the copyright owner for purposes such as criticism, comment, news reporting, education, and parody. The copyright holder's rights are balanced with the public's interest in the work by considering the following four factors: (1) the purpose and character of the use, including its commercial nature; (2) the nature of the copyrighted work; (3) the amount and substantiality of the portion that is used compared to the entire work; and (4) the effect on the potential market for the copyrighted work.

The four fair use factors are applied the same in the on-line context as they would be with a more traditional form of alleged copyright infringement. In L.A. Times v. Free Republic, 54 U.S.P.Q.2d 1453 (C.D. Cal. 2000), a publisher sued the owner and operator of an electronic bulletin board for copying and posting the publisher's news articles on the bulletin board. Although the bulletin board functioned mostly as a site for political commentary, the court rejected the defense of fair use because the amount of copying and the effect on the potential market for the copyrighted work both weighed in favor of protecting the publisher's rights.

WORK-MADE-FOR-HIRE

It is important to recognize that in most cases, the original creator or author of the copyrighted work is the owner of the copyright. If an employee of a company creates the work, the copyright may belong to the company under the work-made-for-hire doctrine of the United States Copyright Act (17 U.S.C. § 201(b)), provided the work is created within the scope of his or her employment. If an independent contractor is hired by the company to develop copyrightable subject matter, the contractor will remain the owner of the copyright unless the parties agree in writing that the work is a work-made-for-hire and that the work fits within certain enumerated categories listed in 17 U.S.C. § 101. To be sure that ownership is transferred, a company should identify, in any agreements with independent contractors, that the resulting work is deemed a work-made-for-hire in accordance with the United States Copyright Act and, if not, that the independent contractor will agree to assign their rights to the company. This issue is of particular importance when an outside contractor is hired to develop a web site. If the hiring company does not get a written assignment from the contractor, the contractor will remain the copyright owner and may prevent the company from hiring a new party to assist in further web site development or modifications, since such activities may infringe the original developer's copyright. Such an assignment of rights should be included in a web site development agreement. If an independent contractor is hired to develop any Internet related technology or other form of intellectual property for a company, the hiring party should consider an assignment of rights as part of their written agreement.

COMMERCIAL TRANSACTIONS

THE EVOLVING RELATIONSHIP OF THE INTERNET AND THE LAW

While there are emerging new uses of the Internet in government, education, science, medicine and the arts, commercial transactions between buyers and sellers are at the heart of Internet growth. These transactions can be business-to-business or business-to-consumer. They can involve any kind of produced goods or services. They can use traditional means of distribution and order fulfillment or new electronic means. Equally important, these transactions, the parties to them and the products involved, can all be subject to regular commercial law principles and, often, to government regulation at federal, state or international levels.

While Internet transactions and the growth of the Internet as a commercial medium of exchange both occur at very high speed, the law moves at a much slower pace. The result is often delay, doubt or confusion as to whether, and how, commercial law or government regulation apply to particular kinds of transactions. Nonetheless, traditional forums of rule making authority have expanded their guidance to the Internet. For example, the Federal Trade Commission now applies more than thirty of its rules and guides to Internet transactions. The Federal Trade Commission has numerous useful publications on its website located at http://www.ftc.gov/bcp/menu-internet.htm.

This state of flux and transition between the law and the Internet means that anyone developing an Internet site for commercial transactions needs to pay careful attention to issues like jurisdiction, taxation, digital signatures, advertising and unsolicited e-mail, privacy and the formation of contracts. These and other subjects are addressed in the sections which follow.

THE INTERNET AND JURISDICTION

The Basis Of Personal Jurisdiction

Businesses operating on the Internet face the possibility that such activities may subject them to liability in other jurisdictions. Since the Internet transcends geographical boundaries, one may be subject to a lawsuit in another state and even in another country.

In the United States, the extent to which one is subject to litigation in other forums is determined by the concept of personal jurisdiction. A court must have personal jurisdiction over the litigants and the claims at issue in order to enter an enforceable judgment. To determine jurisdiction, courts look to the long-arm statute of the state in which litigation is initiated. Most long-arm statutes are similar, and have requirements that the party over which jurisdiction is sought be (1) "transacting business" within the state, (2) "committing a tortious act" within the state, or (3) "committing a tortious act" outside the state that causes injury within the state.

If the long-arm statute is met, the court then must determine whether the exercise of jurisdiction would be consistent with the constitutional requirements of due process. Due process may be satisfied if defendant's contacts with the state are sufficient to give rise to general jurisdiction. If there is no general jurisdiction, specific jurisdiction exists if (i) defendant "purposefully availed" himself/herself of the privilege of acting in the forum state, (ii) the cause of action arose from the defendant's activities in the forum state, and (iii) defendant had sufficient "minimum contacts" with the forum state to make the exercise of jurisdiction "reasonable," i.e., in conformance with notions of "fair play and substantial justice." See, World-Wide Volkswagen Corp. v. Woodson, 444 U.S. 286 (1979).

Personal Jurisdiction And The Internet

Traditional tests of personal jurisdiction are applied to cases involving Internet activity. Presence on the Internet will not automatically subject one to jurisdiction anywhere. Recent cases indicate that merely posting information on a web site with no contact or interaction with the forum state will not subject one to jurisdiction. See Bensusan Restaurant Corp. v. King, 937 F.Supp. 295 (S.D.N.Y. 1996). There must be more. Basically, courts must consider whether messages on a web page that are available to residents of a jurisdiction have been "deliberately directed toward the forum" or have merely arrived there through no direct intention of the defendant.

In a Minnesota case, Minnesota v. Granite Gate Resorts, 568N.W.2d715 (Minn. Ct. App. 1997), the court determined that Minnesota had jurisdiction over an out-of-state company whose web site solicited gambling by Minnesota residents. In *Granite Gate,* a company opened an Internet on-line gambling service from Belize called "WagerNet." In order to access "WagerNet," one first had to pay a $100 set-up fee to receive certain necessary hardware and software. In addition, members were to place at least $1,000 into an account to cover their bets. The WagerNet fee for handling bets was 2-1/2%, and, after paying this fee, one could bet on-line. To attract customers, WagerNet advertised its service on the Internet at the Web site: http://www.vegas.com/wagernet. The web site included several disclaimers and several telephone numbers that prospective members could call to be placed on a mailing list in order to receive information. The Minnesota Attorney General took the position that on-line betting violated both federal law and Minnesota law and filed suit in Minnesota against Granite Gate.

In Granite Gate, the court found that based upon the extent and nature of the Internet advertising, the defendant had sufficient "minimum contacts" with the forum state, and could "reasonably anticipate being hailed into court in Minnesota." The court further held that "maintenance of the suit in the forum state [would not] offend traditional notions of fair play and substantial justice." In reaching its conclusion, the court considered that the Internet advertisement was available "24 hours a day, seven days a week to any Internet user." In addition, the court also considered WagerNet's intent to reach potential customers in Minnesota, as well as the inclusion of numerous Minnesota residents on its mailing list.

Ordinarily, a state's jurisdiction is limited to people, businesses, transactions, events, or other occurrences within the state's geographical territory. A state may, however, exercise its right to assert jurisdiction over non-residents to the extent such parties transact business within the state, commit illegal acts within the state, own or possess real property within the state, make or perform a contract within or connected to the state, breach a fiduciary duty within the state, or do any other act giving rise to personal jurisdiction in accordance with the state's laws. Any business conducting activities through the Internet must therefore assume that it may be subject to jurisdiction in another state. To avoid liability, a business might consider specifically identifying on its web site that its offer is limited to specific states. If the web site merely contains information and is not interactive, it may not provide the minimal contacts necessary to trigger jurisdiction. If, however, direct mailings and toll free telephone numbers are combined with promotion over the Internet, courts may assert jurisdiction. Finally, by incorporating the business activities related to the Internet separately from the company's regular business operations, the business might be able to shield its core assets from liability. Jurisdictional issues related to the Internet are particularly difficult to predict since such cases will depend upon the specific facts and circumstances of each situation. It is fair to say, however, that any company doing business on the Internet should consider that it is now essentially a global business that might be sued in any court and in any territory where its presence becomes known.

The following four themes have emerged from the growing body of case law related to jurisdiction on the Internet:

- **Deriving revenue from forum equals jurisdiction**
  Revenue producing activities on the Internet that result in revenue earned in the forum district may result in a finding of. personal jurisdiction. See CompuServe, Inc. v. Patterson, 89 F.3d 1257 (6th Cir. 1996).

- **Sliding Scale established for Internet sellers**
  The more completely the transaction of business can take place on-line, the more likely that the court will assert jurisdiction based on the on-line activities, Minnesota v. Granite Gate Resorts Inc., 568 N.W.2d 715 (Minn. Ct. App. 1997). Passive web sites that only provide information about the defendant are not likely to be a sufficient basis for personal jurisdiction in a forum state where the defendant does not conduct business. See Cybersell, Inc. v. Cybersell, Inc., 44 U.S.P.Q.2d 1928 (9th Cir. 1997). There are, however, several exceptions where passive Internet sites of out-of-state defendants were found sufficient to establish personal jurisdiction. See Maritz, Inc. v. Cybergold, Inc., 947 F.Supp. 1328 . (E.D. Mo. 1996).

- **Effects test of torts applied**
  The "Effects test" is applied where trademark infringement, defamation, or other torts are alleged, to find jurisdiction based on intentional action expressly aimed at the forum state, and causing harm in the forum state. See Zippo Mfg. Co. v. Zippo Dot Com, Inc., 952 F.Supp. 1119 (W.D. Pa. 1997).

- **24 hours a day-7 days a week**
  The continuous nature of the Internet makes it more substantial than print, radio, or television. As such, Internet commerce or advertising is more likely to increase the amount of contacts with other forums. See Inset Systems, Inc. v. Instruction Set, 937 F.Supp. 161 (D. Conn. 1996).

As online business becomes a global enterprise, cases involving foreign parties and jurisdiction are becoming frequent. The Arista Record Company sued a Spanish business based on a website Puretunes.com that allowed individuals to download copyrighted works owned by Arista without their permission. This action was filed in Washington, D.C. and the Defendant moved for dismissal arguing that the Spanish company had no business contacts in the District of Columbia. During discovery it was revealed that Defendant had customers in the District of Columbia based on information obtained through computer servers owned by a third party service provider as well as the credit card company that provided payment information on customers of the Spanish business. The Motion to Dismiss for lack of personal jurisdiction was therefore denied. See Arista Records Inc. v. Sakfield Holding Company, 314 F.Supp 2nd 27, 71 U.S.P.Q. 2nd 1035 (D.D.C. Apr. 22, 2004).

TAXATION

The increasing amount of commerce conducted through and on the Internet also raises questions of whether and how that commerce should be taxed by the states. With respect to state sales tax laws and the Internet, the closest analogy is the law with respect to mail order (i.e., catalog) sales. In that context, the Supreme Court of the United States has ruled, most recently in Quill Corporation v. North Dakota, 504 U.S. 298 (1992), that a use tax imposed on a mail order firm that was not physically present in that state violated the Commerce clause of the U.S. Constitution. Note that the *Quill* decision is only the most recent of many cases dealing with whether and how a state may legally impose sales and use tax laws on businesses without any employees or property located within that state. Also, it should be noted that the majority opinion in the *Quill* case makes it clear that Congress' power to regulate interstate commerce means that Congress is free to pass legislation overruling the *Quill* decision or any others like it.

With respect to state income taxation of Internet commerce, the closest analogy is the Supreme Court of the United States's 1992 decision in Wisconsin Department of Revenue v. William Wrigley, Jr., Co., (505 U.S. 214). In that case, the Supreme Court was asked to interpret 15 U.S.C. § 381, which prohibits a state from taxing the income of a corporation whose only business activities within the state consist of "solicitation of orders" for tangible goods, provided that the orders are sent outside the state for approval and the goods are delivered from outside that state. At issue in that case were whether the activities in Wisconsin of Wrigley Co.'s sales representatives were so great as to fall outside the protection from tax offered by 15 U.S.C. § 381. The Court found that those representatives' practices of providing free, replacement gum to retailers, of selling gum to retailers, and of storing gum at home or in rented spaces fell outside the statutory protection.

On October 21, 1998, President Clinton signed into law the Internet Tax Freedom Act (ITFA). In November 2001, the ITFA was extended for two years. The ITFA, which expired in 2003, was an effort to preempt state and local taxes that are viewed by some as a potential threat to the growth of commerce on the Internet. The purpose of ITFA was to establish a national policy against state and local government interference with interstate commerce on the Internet by establishing a moratorium on the imposition of taxes that interfere with the free flow of commerce on the Internet. On December 3, 2004 President Bush signed the Internet Tax Nondiscrimination Act into law reinstating the ban on Internet access taxes for an additional three years.

As more and more businesses are looking at the Internet as a vehicle for selling products, there will be continued discussion as to whether the imposition of new efforts to collect government taxes will hinder electronic commerce. In the meantime, according to Forrester Research, Inc., on-line retail sales have exploded past $100 billion in 2003. This represents an increase from $500 million in 1995, $1.1 billion in 1996, and $6 billion in 1997 and $14.8 billion in 2000. On-line retail sales are expected to reach $269 billion in 2005. It should be noted, however, that Internet sales still represent only a small fraction of retail sales (less 6%). Whether or not the freedom from taxation for on-line commerce is justified or poses a significant threat to traditional retail businesses remains a significant issue.

ELECTRONIC PAYMENT SYSTEMS

While the conventional form of payment for retail products and services includes coins and currency, checks, money orders, and credit cards, there are also electronic fund transfer systems that have been used for over a decade including automated teller machines, debit cards used to automatically pay merchants by debiting customer's accounts, and point of sale systems which debit or credit customer accounts. There are a number of federal laws which apply to any entity providing such services including the Truth in Lending Act ("TILA") and the Electronic Fund Transfer Act ("EFTA"). The TILA and the EFTA protect consumers with paper-less transactions involving telephones, electronics, and computers. Other federal laws address financial privacy issues related to electronic cash payment systems including the Right to Financial Privacy Act of 1978.

Rapidly developing electronic cash technologies may challenge the traditional banking rules and regulations. It is not yet clear how these new technologies might mesh with existing payment systems and what laws will control. Legal issues concerning bank regulations, consumer protection, financial privacy and risk allocation all must be considered by any business that is considering utilizing some form of electronic cash payment technology.

The newer electronic cash payment systems store monetary value in the form of electronic signals on a plastic card, on a computer drive or on a disk. There are also digital cash systems which allow electronic cash to be used over computer networks without use of a plastic card - sometimes called "digital cash." An example of a digital cash transaction would be as follows:

1. A digital cash account is opened by a customer by depositing funds in a "Cyberbank."

2. The customer's funds are held in trust by the Cyberbank.

3. When the customer purchases a product or service over the

Internet, the customer transmits an encrypted electronic e-mail message with the customer's unique digital signature to the Cyberbank requesting release of customer's funds.

4. The customer's account is debited and the digital cash is transmitted via phone lines to the customer's computer.

5. The customer then transmits the digital cash to the merchant who can verify authenticity of the customer's digital signature, credit the digital cash amount to merchant's account with the Cyberbank, or transmit the digital cash to another party.

6. The Cyberbank may charge the customer or merchant a fee to participate in such an electronic payment system.

The Federal Reserve Board's Regulation "E" governs on-line payment systems which provide digital substitutes for cash and electronic funds transfers. This federal law defines electronic funds transfers as any transfer of funds initiated through an electronic terminal, telephone, computer, or magnetic tape for the purpose of ordering, instructing, or authorizing a financial institution to debit or credit an account. A business contemplating use of such an online payment system should verify that it complies with the requirements of Regulation "E."

SELLING PRODUCTS ON AUCTION SITES

Businesses of all sizes are finding avenues to use the Internet to market their products. One of the more recent trends, especially for smaller businesses, is the use of Internet auction sites for both sale and purchase of products. There are two main types of Internet auctions. In an ascending price auction (often referred to as a "forward" or "English" auction); a seller puts up product for sale on the seller's own site or an Internet "marketplace" site, and bidders place bids in ascending amounts. After a pre-determined time, the top bidder pays the seller, completes the transaction and the product is shipped. In a descending price auction (often referred to as a "reverse" or "Dutch" auction), a buyer announces its product needs on its own or an Internet "marketplace" site and sellers submit their lowest price. After a pre-determined time, the seller selects the lowest bid, completes the transaction and the product is shipped.

Most auction sites have a method whereby buyers can rate sellers and sellers can rate buyers. Sellers are prohibited from placing false testimonials in their auctions. Sellers must also refrain from placing bids on their own products to increase the price. As reported on the Federal Trade Commission's web site, "(t)hese practices are not only unethical, they're also fraudulent." Sellers also may not offer illegal items through Internet Auctions. The Federal Trade Commission provides additional details to protect sellers and buyers at www.ftc.gov/bcp/conline/pubs/onlin/auctions.htm.

SECURITY ON-LINE AND DIGITAL SIGNATURES

A major concern of buyers and sellers over the Internet involves the security and authenticity of transactions conducted on-line. How can the seller be assured of the integrity of the orders and payments for its products and services? How can the buyer be assured it will be provided the quality product or service purchased on-line?

Digital signatures and third party certification are methods used by vendors to authenticate the buyer. A "digital signature" is the electronic substitute for a handwritten signature. The Minnesota Electronic Authentication Act, Minn. Stat. §325K.01 et. seq., defines digital signatures as "a transformation of a message using an asymmetric cryptosystem such that a person having the initial messages and the signer's public key can accurately determine: (1) whether the transformation was created using the private key that corresponds to the signer's public key; and (2) whether the initial message has been altered since the transformation was made." An asymmetric cryptosystem is "an algorithm or series of algorithms that provide a secure key pair."

In addition, Minnesota has enacted the Uniform Electronic Transactions Act (Minnesota Statutes Chapter 325L, as added by

Chapter 371 of the 2000 Laws of Minnesota) (UETA). Under Chapter 325L, parties may choose (but are not required) to use electronic records or signatures in place of written ones. (Note that the UETA does not apply, among other instances, to transactions governed by certain sections of the Uniform Commercial Code). The UETA provides that electronic records or signatures may not be denied validity or legal effect solely because they are in electronic form, and that such records or signatures satisfy laws that require records or signatures to be in writing. The UETA also contains provisions:

- setting out requirements for accessing, reading and retaining electronic records and signatures;
- allowing for the notarization of electronic records and signatures, and the transferability of electronic records;
- addressing when electronic records are considered to be received and sent; and
- allowing for making changes to already-transmitted electronic records (including but not limited to when those records contain errors).

Digital signatures should become a viable means of creating legally binding contracts for products and services on-line. Utah and Minnesota are among the first states to enact a digital signature act, and other states are likely to follow. A key element in the use of digital signatures involves a form of encryption. An individual is given two encryption keys - a private key known only to the individual and a public key made available to other Internet users. The sender of a message on-line uses his or her unique private key as well as the public key of the intended recipient of the on-line message. The recipient of the on-line message must use the public key of the sender and the unique private key of the recipient to receive the on-line message. For many transactions on the Internet, the digital signatures resulting from this public key encryption system will provide adequate security. There is also an encryption system involving a third party which can certify the identity of the seller or recipient for purposes of authenticating the message or payment. The use of such third party digital certification systems may help further address some of the legal concerns relative to authentication of electronic transactions. Rules and standards for such third party certification are still evolving and some uncertainty remains regarding liability of such third parties for non-payment or errors in the certification process. Courts are likely to look at existing laws covering liability for credit card transactions when considering liability of third parties providing digital certification.

UNSOLICITED E-MAIL

Bulk e-mail has become a popular way to market products or services on-line. With minimal cost and quick delivery, e-mail has been adopted as a cheap and effective direct marketing tool. However, the use of bulk e-mail has also become an annoyance and hindrance to many users of the Internet and has led to proposed federal legislation to try to curb such practices. Of particular concern is what is known as "spamming." This is the Internet equivalent of junk mail and consists of a wide distribution of unsolicited e-mail messages usually promoting a product or service. In one case, Cyber Promotions, Inc. v. America On-Line, Inc., C.A. No. 96-2486 (E.D. Pa. Nov. 4, 1996), the Court found that Cyber Promotions, which had been sending bulk e-mail messages to AOL subscribers, did not have a First Amendment right of free speech to deliver unsolicited e-mail through a privately owned computer services network such as AOL and that AOL was entitled to restrict the transmission of bulk e-mail messages to its customers. The AOL electronic community was not deemed a public forum that would allow the exercise of such First Amendment rights. In a related case, CompuServe Inc. v. Cyber Promotions, Inc., 962 F. Supp. 1015 (S.D. Ohio 1997), the Court found that the disseminator of bulk e-mail may be liable for damages as a result of trespass on the computer system of the Internet service provider if such e-mail transmissions are received without the consent of the Internet service provider.

THE CAN-SPAM ACT

The CAN-SPAM Act (acronym for "Controlling the Assault of Non-solicited Pornography and Marketing") (P.L. 108-187, 117 Stat. 2719) became effective January 1, 2004. This new federal law preempts over 30 state laws (including the Minnesota law) that had been enacted to control the proliferation of unsolicited commercial e-mail. CAN-SPAM does not ban unsolicited commercial e-mail but may have a significant impact on all businesses who use e-mail to communicate with or advertise to customers. The federal law leaves intact those portions of state laws that cover falsified information and other fraudulent activity. CAN-SPAM applies to all commercial electronic mail, defined as any electronic mail message the primary purpose of which is the commercial advertisement or promotion of a commercial product or service. So called "transaction and relationship" messages are specifically excluded and include e-mail sent with billing statements, emails necessary to complete a transaction, warranty information, account balance, and similar type information. The law requires that all commercial e-mail messages include 1) text that describes how the recipient can "opt out" of receiving future e-mails; 2) the senders physical address; and 3) an indication that the e-mail is a solicitation. The law also bans the use of a false or misleading header, sender or subject line information or the use of deceptive subject headings.

Any business that is contemplating sending bulk e-mail must consider all federal and state laws which may apply. This legal landscape is likely to change at any time. Permission should be obtained from any Internet service provider that would be the recipient of such bulk e-mail messages. Permission should also be requested from the ultimate recipient of such bulk e-mail with an opportunity to opt out of receiving such messages. Under no circumstances should any false or misleading information be transmitted on-line. The volume of e-mail messages should be reasonable so as not to become an annoyance or hindrance to the recipients. Finally, the terms of an agreement with an Internet service provider may specifically restrict the use of bulk e-mail.

PRIVACY

Since the Internet involves the transmission of large amounts of data among and between a large number of people and organizations, privacy of such data is of great concern. This problem has been widely discussed and debated and is likely going to grow in intensity as the collection and communication of personal data continues to increase. However, this is not an entirely new phenomenon.

Even before the Internet existed, laws were enacted to protect individuals from the use and disclosure of personal information. The Electronic Fund Transfer Act passed in 1978 required financial institutions to disclose the circumstances under which they would provide account information on individuals to third parties. The Cable Privacy Act, Electronic Communications Privacy Act (ECPA), and the Telephone Consumer Protection Act were all designed to protect individuals from unreasonable intrusions on the personal privacy of individuals.

Because privacy flows from constitutional, tort, legislative, and public perceptions, it is difficult to provide general legal guidance as to how such issues might be handled by the courts. It should be noted, however, that corporations do not have a right to privacy. A corporation must therefore rely upon the intellectual property and unfair competition laws.

The United States Constitution limits the ability of the government to obtain private information about individuals. These constitutional protections are, however, limited to government intrusion into personal privacy and do not cover circumstances where an individual voluntarily places personal information into commercial use or makes such information accessible to another party.

The ECPA covers some of the basic privacy issues surrounding the use of e-mail, including the procedural steps necessary to search and retrieve such information.

Privacy issues on the Internet may differ depending upon the product, parties, method of collecting information, use of the information, and storage medium involved in the collection and use of information.

For example, there are federal privacy laws which cover government record keeping (5 U.S.C. § 552); videotape rental records (18 U.S.C. § 2710); credit reports (15 U.S.C. § 1681); political contributors (2 U.S.C. § 438); tax records (26 U.S.C. § 6103); cable TV viewing habits (47 U.S.C. § 551); and delivery of pornography through the mail (39 U.S.C. § 3008).

The ECPA regulates the privacy of e-mail messages in public e-mail systems by prohibiting the interception, use, or disclosure of e-mail by third parties. The ECPA also sets forth procedural safeguards and standards that law enforcement agencies must follow when seeking access to e-mail. The ECPA does not apply if a party has consented to such monitoring, and it may not apply to private e-mail systems such as those operated by employers. Most businesses and organizations that have implemented e-mail systems have also developed corporate policies which specifically clarify the scope of privacy, if any, employees are entitled to within the employer's system. (See the section of this Guide entitled Employment Law - Privacy of Employee E-mail).

In USA vs. Bradford Councilman, 373 F. 3rd 197 (1st Cir. 2004); 2004 WL 1453032, the First Circuit United States Court of Appeals determined that there was no violation of the Wire Tap Act as amended by the Electronic Communications Privacy Act (ECPA) when stored e-mail was accessed, because, since it was in storage, no "interception" occurred within the meaning of the federal laws. The defendant was an officer of a business that operated an online listing service for rare and out of print books. The business also provided e-mail service to some of its customers who were book dealers. The government claimed that the business developed and used computer code that enabled them to intercept, copy and store e-mail messages that were being transmitted from Amazon.com to their book dealer customers and to obtain commercial advantage by reading these messages prior to them being received by the intended recipients. Defendants argued successfully that since the definition "electronic communication" in the statute makes no reference to stored communications no "interception" can occur while the e-mails are in electronic storage. Since there is no illegal interception as defined by the law the defendant argued there was no violation of the federal law. The case demonstrates the difficulty in application of these older federal wiretap laws to more recent Internet based technology as the court states "the language [of the statute] may be out of step with the technological realities of computer crimes. However, it is not the province of this court to graft meaning onto the statute where Congress has spoken plainly." A strongly worded dissent suggests that the narrow approach of this court renders the Wiretap Act irrelevant.

It is important for businesses to notify their employees that their e-mails may be monitored and the employees have no right to privacy to such communications. Employers might even request that their employees sign a statement acknowledging that the employer has the right to monitor, access, and disclose any e-mail messages received or transmitted on their system. Such policy should be clear and unambiguous and, once implemented, applied by the employer consistently and fairly.

The Federal Trade Commission (FTC) brought an enforcement action targeted at the privacy practices of a web site operated by Geocities. The FTC accused Geocities of deceptive trade practices in its collection and use of personal information obtained from web site visitors. Geocities used an on-line application for new members and sold the collected information to third-party marketers. The FTC claimed that Geocities misrepresented that the collected information was used only for specific advertising offers requested by members. In a consent order, Geocities agreed to post a clear and prominent "Privacy Notice" which would disclose what information is being collected, for what purposes, to whom the information will be disclosed, and how consumers can access the information. Parental consent is necessary before collecting information from children under 13 years old and

Geocities must give members the opportunity to have their information deleted from Geocities' and third party's databases, In The Matter Of Geocities, Federal Trade Commission File No. 9823015, August 13, 1998 (consent order is available at http://www.ftc.gov/ os/1998/08/goe-ord.htm).

PRIVACY ISSUES IN EUROPE

The European Community has gone far beyond the United States in its efforts to protect privacy rights. A Directive passed by the European Parliament in November 1995 requires that, among other things, personal data can only be processed if the subject has granted "unambiguous consent" to the collection and disclosure and use of the information. Article 25 of the Directive specifically covers the transfer of personal data from European Union countries to countries outside of the European Union and only allows transfers of personal data to those countries which afford an adequate level of protection for privacy of data or if adequate safeguards are implemented, i.e. contracts to specifically protect and preserve the data. It is still not clear whether the United States will be deemed adequate for purposes of the transfer of personal data from European Union countries in accordance with Article 25. The transfer of personal data to the United States from Europe will likely be evaluated based upon the federal, state, and local privacy laws in effect as well as any specific contractual arrangements that are in place to protect and preserve the specific data at issue.

Any business, large or small, doing business on the Internet must consider itself a global business, and the impact of the European privacy initiative may have an effect on their operations. The collection of data on-line to enhance marketing or advertising may be an acceptable practice in the United States but falls under the more severe restrictions that protect such personal data in Europe.

MINNESOTA INTERNET PRIVACY AND COMMERCIAL E-MAIL LAWS

On May 22, 2002, Minnesota enacted two laws related to Internet privacy and commercial e-mail solicitation, otherwise known as anti-spam legislation, which become effective March 1, 2003. The Internet privacy portion of the law (Minn. Stat. 325 M.01-325M.09) is designed to restrict the ability of an Internet service provider to disclose "personally identifiable information" including e-mail addresses, phone numbers, online contact viewing habits, and browsing history to third parties. The law provides limited exceptions for such disclosure and sets forth specific requirements for obtaining authorization. Violators of the law can be sued for $500 or actual damages for each violation.

The anti-spam law provision (Minn. Stat. 325F.694) has been preempted by the Federal CAN-SPAM Act discussed earlier.

CONTRACTS

SALES MODELS

It is important to remember that most of the current commercial transactions on the Internet, and most of the anticipated transaction growth, occur as business-to-consumer sales. In such cases, the selling business wants to create on the Internet a virtual storefront allowing for anytime sale of products.

It is also important to remember that most of the earlier models of electronic commerce involved business-to-business transactions using electronic data interchange. In that model, a producer of goods, for example a parts supplier to an original equipment manufacturer, would negotiate via traditional means (meetings, mail, phone, fax) a trading partner agreement providing for terms of ordering, sale, delivery, payment, returns, warranties and the like. This agreement manifested the intent of the parties to contract and to be bound by the terms of the agreement. The mechanics of the transaction - ordering and payment, for example - were then done electronically (originally by proprietary system, and more recently, via the Internet).

Since the on-line business-to-consumer seller wants to reach the largest possible audience, and wants to make the transaction as constraint-free as possible, such sellers sometimes try to avoid having any terms and conditions of use or transaction displayed at their Internet site. In this view, web site design makes the purpose of the site clear: to offer to sell a particular product. When the consumer enters his credit card and clicks on a sale indicator, that consumer is giving his acceptance of the transaction and approval for payment. The major contract elements of offer, acceptance and consideration are met. While there are good reasons for even a virtual storefront seller of hard goods to have terms and conditions of use and sale (it aids, for example, in "branding" the site), it is useful from a liability avoidance position to have web site disclaimers and notices. For example, warranties, remedies, restrictions on use (if any), or limitations of liability should also be considered when creating an on-line contract. What, if any, negotiation of terms can be accomplished on-line? These contract issues and terms of use notices are even more important when the transaction involves contracts for the on-line licensing and distribution of digital products like software, music, video or text.

ON-LINE SOFTWARE LICENSING

There are some key issues for any business to consider relative to on-line distribution of software or other products.

- How can you be assured that the person you are dealing with is that person?
- How do you authenticate and avoid repudiation?
- How do you avoid electronic forgery?
- How do you confirm integrity of information shared on-line?
- How to preserve confidentiality?
- How can you enforce the terms of the contract?
- How do you preserve evidence in case of future disputes?

Software vendors are now both marketing and actually distributing software on-line. The more common approach, however, still remains ordering of the software product over the Internet or by telephone with hard copies delivered to the user. This off-line arrangement may be more convenient than on-line delivery, which may require users to download the software onto tangible media themselves. Off-line distribution also avoids any on-line technical delivery problems. Trade secret protection may also be lost if delivered on-line without any encryption. For this reason, many vendors still utilize the Internet to market their software products and not for actual distribution.

Businesses that use online distribution should consider writing a procedure guideline for distributing software online. Topics of this guideline may include procedures for monitoring the Internet for pirated copies of their software, devising a method to encrypt the software with registration material that makes the software inoperable without registration, and effectively writing licensing terms.

Enforceable Click-On Licenses

If contemplating on-line distribution, it is essential to have an enforceable on-line agreement with the end user to protect valuable intellectual property rights and minimize any potential risk and liability. The Electronic Signatures in Global and National Commerce Act (E-Sign) is a step forward for ensuring the enforceability of these agreements. The Act encourages businesses and consumers to contract and communicate electronically with electronic signatures, contracts, and other electronic records. Enacted October 1, 2000, E-Sign gives electronic transactions the same validity as their paper-based counterparts.

With E-Sign, an electronic signature is defined as "an electronic sound, symbol, or process attached to or logically associated with a contract or other record and executed or adopted by a person with the intent to sign the record." Therefore, clicking "YES" or "I AGREE", placing a name in a form box on a web site, or signing an e-mail can legally bind the individual performing the action. Because of the near instantaneous actions of electronic transactions, however, E-Sign also provides consumer protections that businesses should acknowledge. Business guidelines to remain in step with these protections are discussed in the Security On-line and Digital Signatures section of this Guide.

In addition to E-Sign, courts have upheld the validity of on-line licensing agreements. In Compuserve Inc. v. Patterson, 89 F.3d

1257 (6th Cir. 1996), the Court found an electronic agreement enforceable when a Texas lawyer entered into an on-line agreement for distribution of the lawyer's software products. The Court concluded that typing the word "AGREE" in response to prompts generated by a "point-and-click contract" on-line, the individual "manifested assent" to the terms of the license agreement. This case supports the enforceability of on-line licenses, especially if they are designed to require the other party to acknowledge acceptance through some affirmative act, such as clicking on a mouse to indicate acceptance of the terms and conditions of the license. In ProCD Inc. v. Zeidenberg 86 F.3d 1447 (7th Cir. 1996), the Court found a "shrink-wrap" license enforceable. In ProCD the license was encoded on the CD-Rom disks, printed in the manual, and appeared on the users screen every time the program was run. In a breach of warranty case involving a software license similar to that in *ProCD* the Supreme Court of Washington deemed it enforcible, M.A. Mortenson Co. Inc. v. Timberline Software Corp. 998 P2d 305 (Wash. 2000). A fourth case, Hotmail Corp. v. Van $ Money Pie, Inc., 47 U.S.P.Q. 2d 1020 (N.D.Cal. 1998) appears to confirm the enforceability of "point-and-click" contracts on the Internet. The Hotmail Terms of Services Agreement is available at http://www.hotmail.com.

Businesses that use on-line licensing should be aware, however, that the mere placement of licensing terms on a web site may be insufficient to create a binding agreement. In Specht v. Netscape Communications Corp., 306 F.3d 17 (2nd Cir. 2002), the Court found that licensing terms found below the download area on a web page were not binding on visitors who downloaded software. Visitors could download the software without examining the terms if they did not scroll down the browser. The Court considered the terms a "browse-wrap" agreement and found that they did not constitute binding assent. Businesses should require consumers to affirmatively accept licensing terms before they are given access to downloading software. Not all courts have enforced shrinkwrap or so-called "click on" licenses. In Klocek v. Gateway, Inc. 104 F. Supp. 2d 1332 (D.Kan. 2000) the Court did not follow *ProCD* and held that the plaintiff computer purchaser did not agree to the license terms.

The Court determined that the buyer was the offeror and the vendor accepted buyer's offer when it shipped the computer in response to the offer. Even if the license enclosed in the box stated additional or different terms, unless acceptance of those terms was a condition of buyer's acceptance and vendor provided no unwillingness to proceed, the license terms were not enforceable against the buyer.

In Bowers v. Baystate Technologies, 64 USPQ2d 1065 (Fed. Cir. 2002) a prohibition against reverse engineering contained in a shrinkwrap software license was enforced against the defendant purchaser. Citing *ProCD* and Massachusetts contract law, the Court rejected the defendant's arguments that the United States Copyright Act preempted the reverse engineering prohibition and that the license itself was not enforceable.

Forcing the end user to go through a sequence of steps before being permitted to access or download software allows the merchant the ability to put together a "click on" license that contains appropriate warranty disclaimers, limitations of liability, and other necessary licensing provisions as well as registration information. It would be difficult for end users to argue that they did not review or acknowledge acceptance of the license terms if they are required to go through such process prior to downloading the software. Obviously, it is important to have end users click on a "buy" or "download" button only after the license terms and conditions have been accepted by the end user. This process can avoid the lack of notice problems encountered in the typical shrink-wrap transactions. The click-on license agreement can be short and simple or more comprehensive depending upon the specific objectives of the merchant.

Essential Steps In On-Line Distribution

The following are essential steps in implementing any on-line distribution process:

- The user should receive some notification prior to buying or downloading the software that it is subject to a license agreement.
- The user should be required to review the license terms prior to any buy or download option.
- The user should be given the option to abandon the download or buy sequence at any point during the transaction.
- The license agreement itself should be short, simple and easily understood.
- The license terms should be prepared for the particular software application and particular use contemplated.
- It is also important to register the end users and obtain basic information including name and address for billing and future support (if any). Such registration must be completed prior to any buy or download of the software.
- Finally, the merchant should make sure that it utilizes the appropriate copyright and trademark notices in any on-screen displays.

Click-On License Terms

On-line software licenses can and should be as short and simple as possible. Although the needs of the particular business should be addressed, some of the basic terms which would appear in any such license agreement include the following boilerplate terms:

> **Merger Clause.** "This agreement constitutes the entire agreement between the parties pertaining to the subject matter hereof, and supersedes any and all written and oral

agreements previously existing between the parties with respect to such subject matter."

Governing Law. "This agreement shall be governed by the laws of the State of Minnesota, excluding (1) that body of law known as conflicts of law, and (2) the United Nations Convention for Contracts for the International Sale of Goods."

Unless the parties to a contract agree otherwise, a merchant that regularly deals in the type of goods being sold impliedly warrants that the goods will be fit for the ordinary purposes for which the goods are used and that they are fit for the particular purpose for which they are intended. These warranties are typically disclaimed in software license agreements. The enforceability of warranty disclaimers and limitations of liability may, however, be subject to the Magnuson Moss Warranty Federal Trade Commission Improvement Act ("Act") (15 U.S.C. §2301), which applies to consumer products presented to consumers. It is therefore important that the disclaimers include language that complies with the Act.

<u>LIMITATION OF LIABILITY</u>. IN NO EVENT WILL VENDOR BE LIABLE TO YOU FOR ANY LOST PROFITS, LOST SAVINGS, OR ANY OTHER INCIDENTAL, INDIRECT, SPECIAL OR CONSEQUENTIAL DAMAGES, ARISING OUT OF YOUR USE OR INABILITY TO USE THE SOFTWARE EVEN IF ADVISED OF THE POSSIBILITY OF SUCH DAMAGES. SOME STATES DO NOT ALLOW THE LIMITATION OR EXCLUSION OF LIABILITY FOR INCIDENTAL OR CONSEQUENTIAL DAMAGES SO THE ABOVE LIMITATION OR EXCLUSION MAY NOT APPLY TO YOU.

<u>DISCLAIMER OF WARRANTIES</u>. THIS PRODUCT IS PROVIDED "AS IS" WITHOUT WARRANTY OF ANY KIND, EITHER EXPRESS OR IMPLIED, INCLUDING, BUT NOT LIMITED TO, THE IMPLIED WARRANTIES OF

MERCHANTABILITY, FITNESS FOR A PARTICULAR PURPOSE, TITLE, OR NON-INFRINGEMENT. SOME JURISDICTIONS DO NOT ALLOW THE EXCLUSION OF IMPLIED WARRANTIES, SO THE ABOVE EXCLUSION MAY NOT APPLY TO YOU.

A governmental agency might assert greater rights to use of software unless otherwise restricted by the license. One way to limit such rights is to include the following proviso:

Restrictive Rights Legend. Any Software which is downloaded from this Server for or on behalf of the United States of America, its agencies and/or instrumentalities ("U.S. government"), is provided with restrictive rights. Use, duplication, or disclosure by the U.S. government is subject to restrictions as set forth in subparagraph (c)(1)(ii) of the Rights in Technical Data and Computer Software Clause at DFARS 252.227-7013 or subparagraphs (c)(1)and (2) of the Commercial Computer Software-Restricted Rights at 48 CFR 52.227-19, as applicable. The manufacturer is ____________________.

Payment

In addition to the issue of enforceability of the license agreement, the vendor should also consider how payments will be made for the software product. As businesses continue to jump on the Internet bandwagon, there has been more concern in developing a secure and reliable method of payment. A fundamental issue with making on-line transactions secure is that information transmitted over the Internet can be intercepted and copied. Fraudulent use of such numbers or passwords continues to be a concern. Some of the current approaches to secure payment include the use of (1) third party confirmation such as credit cards, (2) electronic money or smart cards, or (3) digital cash. A more direct method of secure payments on-line is through the use of encryption and a secure server with Secure Socket Layer protection. This allows for authentication of customers, confidentiality of price information, and delivery of trade secret software. Unfortunately, U.S. export controls remain somewhat restrictive with respect to file encryption features and even the use of encryption has not been immune from hackers. Netscape has already seen its encryption key discovered by graduate students at the University of California at Berkeley. For more discussion of electronic payment or encryption see the Commercial Transactions section, Electronic Payment Systems And Security Online And Digital Signatures.

Electronic Data Interchange

Electronic data interchange (or EDI) has been in existence for some time and detailed trading partner agreements can avoid many of the costs and concerns in doing business on-line via EDI. Basically, EDI is the same as an e-mail with the addition of a command structure set for automatic processing. E-Sign, discussed above, validates EDI in that electronic transactions are given the same validity as paper documents. A model EDI agreement is available from the American Bar Association. You can order a copy of *The Commercial Use of Electronic Data Interchange: A Report and Model Trading Partner Agreement* from the American Bar Association at 312/988-5522.

WEB SITE DISCLAIMERS AND NOTICES

It is important to include web site disclaimers. Disclaimers put visitors on notice and are essential to limiting the liability of the web site owner. As with other disclaimers, web site disclaimers should be easy to find and easy to understand. Often, the disclaimers are listed on a separate legal page.

If using a web site legal page, there are certain considerations to keep in mind. First, if the disclaimer is significant and seriously affects your liability, that disclaimer should be placed alongside the appropriate text and not buried in the legal page. Second, there should be a notice on the home page that legal restrictions apply to the web site, and visitors should be directed to the legal page before proceeding beyond the home page. There should be a warning that they will be bound by the terms and conditions contained on the web site legal page and that they shouldn't proceed without a visit to the legal page. Third, the web site legal page should be clear and easy to read and as formal as appropriate. Finally, one may consider requiring web site visitors to indicate their acceptance of the terms and conditions in a clear and unambiguous way such as by clicking on an "Accept" button. See the discussion above concerning enforceability of "point and click" license agreements.

The following is a list of disclaimers that should be listed on any web site.

Restrict Permissible Uses Of Web Site Materials

There should be a warning that prohibits the reproduction, distribution, or retransmission by visitors of any materials posted at the web site without the prior permission of the web site owner. One right that can be granted to web site visitors is the right to download a copy of the materials for personal non-commercial home use.

Provide Copyright And Trademark Notices

Copyright notices should be placed wherever appropriate on a web site. Copyright notices alert visitors that their rights to use the material are limited which make it impossible for violators to later assert a defense of innocent infringement. Also, copyright notices are often essential in foreign countries. Trademark notices alert visitors that their rights to use the symbols and characters at the web site are limited. Also, Federal trademark law requires active policing of the trademark and failure to stop unauthorized users can result in "abandonment" of a federally registered mark.

Limit Open-Ended Liability For Damages

As discussed above, businesses must place reasonable limitations on potentially open-ended liability. One suggested method is to limit the types of damages that may be sought by web site visitors. For example, a web site owner should exclude liability for consequential damages incurred by web site visitors. Another way to limit liability is to impose a cap on damages. Caps, however, must be reasonable in order to be enforceable.

Consumer protection laws restrict the ability to limit liability under certain circumstances. Also, if conducting electronic commerce, the Federal Trade Commission requires that any liability limitations be accompanied by a warning that such limitations may not apply in certain jurisdictions.

Disclaim Responsibility For Errors And Omissions In Web Site Materials

Businesses should warn that the information on the web site might include inaccuracies and out-of-date information and should require that use of such information be at the web site visitor's own risk. Also, businesses should further provide that all documents, audio, video, software and other data are provided "as is" without warranty of any kind. If conducting electronic commerce, this provision should be carefully drafted to reference any applicable warranty provided in a separate license or other document.

Disclaim All Implied Warranties

Businesses should disclaim all warranties implied by law, especially in situations involving software. For example, the implied warranty of merchantability would guarantee that material delivered by the web site owner is consistent with "quality standards in the trade." The ability to disclaim implied warranties is also restricted by consumer protection laws. If conducting electronic commerce, the Federal Trade Commission mandates that any liability limitations be accompanied by a warning that such limitations may not apply in certain jurisdictions.

Disclaim Responsibility For Material Posted At Linked Sites

The law is unclear as to whether a web site owner can be vicariously liable for material on sites to which it is linked. The most prudent course is to disclose to web site visitors that the web site owner does not regularly review materials posted on the sites to which it is linked, that the web site owner does not necessarily endorse all of the materials appearing on such linked sites, and that any decision of web site visitors to view any of the linked web sites is at their own risk. Businesses should also consider the laws of the state. Linking to sites containing gambling, lottery, pornography, and any other sites that may be unlawful may subject a business to an unwanted lawsuit.

WEB SITE DEVELOPMENT AND/OR WEB HOSTING AGREEMENT

An interesting and inviting web site can serve as a powerful marketing tool. The design and implementation of a web site usually requires the services of an outside contractor experienced in web site development. It is essential to have an agreement that clearly addresses a variety of issues both to the web site developer and the business. Sound contracting principles should be followed in the preparation of any such agreement so both parties clearly understand the obligations and allocation of responsibilities. Some of the issues that should be considered when pursuing such an arrangement and preparing the appropriate agreement are as follows:

- What is the purpose of the web site?
- Will the business, the developer, or a third party serve as host of the site?
- Will goods, services, or information be sold on-line?
- How much will it cost to develop and maintain the site?
- What are the actual and projected fees for the development and ongoing support and maintenance of the site?
- Has the business considered a number of different web site developers and hosts?
- What special programs or features are important to the business? What programming languages will be used to develop and implement the site (HTML, VRML, Java, Pearl, C++, Visual Basic, ASP, Flash, etc.)?

- What if a new provider of web site hosting or related services is to be hired by the business? Can the web site be easily transported to another host? Can the business or other service provider easily continue to maintain or support the site?
- Who is responsible for obtaining rights to any third party materials and other content used in the site?
- Who retains intellectual property rights associated with the web site including any patents, copyrights, or trademarks?
- What limitations of liability, indemnification, and termination provisions are included?
- What remedies are available for failed performance? Are there reasonable warranties and representations?
- Is training included?
- Who is responsible for obtaining the domain name?
- Who is responsible for listing the web site with various search engines? Is the responsibility a one-time occurrence or continuous?
- Is the web site compatible with all appropriate web browsers?
- What is expected from the site and from the developer who is constructing the site?
- What is the expected up time and response time?
- Are e-mail, file transfer protocol, e-commerce, statistics or other capabilities included?

APPLICATION OF THE UNIFORM COMMERCIAL CODE TO THE INTERNET AND THE UNIFORM COMPUTER INFORMATION TRANSACTIONS ACT

Software and information vendors may want to review the enforceability of their computer software or information related licenses including shrink-wrap or click-on licenses in light of a proposed new uniform law.

The Uniform Commercial Code or U.C.C. has been adopted in virtually every state and provides legal guidance concerning contract formation, terms, and remedies. There have been efforts to adapt Article 2 of the U.C.C., which covers sales of goods, to more specifically address issues concerning computer software, information, and other technology products and services, as well as considerations for electronic commerce. For years, committees of the National Conference of Commissioners on Uniform State Laws ("NCCUSL"), the American Law Institute ("ALI"), the American Bar Association, and other groups have examined the possibility of creating a new article to the U.C.C. that would address an alleged mismatch between the U.C.C. aimed at the sale of tangible goods and new contract relationships in which information or intangibles were the focus of the transaction.

On April 7, 1999 the ALI and NCCUSL announced that they were abandoning their efforts to jointly promulgate a new Article 2(b) for the U.C.C. Instead, NCCUSL moved ahead by itself and independently issued rules for such transactions in a freestanding uniform act called the Uniform Computer Information Transactions Act (UCITA). The UCITA was officially adopted by NCCUSL on July 29, 1999.

The UCITA is the first uniform law that would govern software licenses and has sections related to the enforceability of shrink-wrap and click-on licenses and establishes rules for what law governs, how to create electronic contracts, and what default rules apply to contracts created on-line. The UCITA still follows general principles of contract law. It represents a movement towards licensing of information and away from the sale of copies. Thus a vendor may retain more control over the product. Some critics have suggested that there is no need for such new law. While the UCITA has many supporters, it has also been characterized by some as a confusing statute with over 335 pages of text and reporter's notes. One of the concerns involves the UCITA's use of "manifestation of assent after opportunity to review" as the touchstone for contract formation relative to shrink-wrap and click-on license agreements. The UCITA requires that there be an opportunity to review and reject license terms before payment and delivery, with a right to a refund if the terms are not acceptable.

UCITA also provides new warranty rules for software including a new implied warranty of merchantability (the program is "fit for the ordinary purposes for which such computer programs are used").

NCCUSL is an organization of lawyers, professors, and judges who draft proposals for uniform and model laws such as UCITA and then work towards their enactment at state legislatures. The UCITA will likely be presented to the Minnesota state legislature for consideration and possible enactment. However, the Minnesota Attorney General has opposed enactment of the UCITA and the Minnesota NCCUSL representatives voted against the implementation of the law. In the meantime, knowledge and understanding of the UCITA and its provisions are essential to anyone interested in the preparation of enforceable software and related licenses. For more information on the UCITA, see http://www.ucitaonline.com or www.nccusl.org.

A website has also been established by an organization opposed to UCITA known as Americans for Fair Electronic Commerce Transactions (AFFECT). For information on why some groups oppose UCITA see www.ucita.com.

EMPLOYMENT LAW

The Internet affects the relationships between employers and employees. E-mail communication has become commonplace as a fast and easy method of communication between employees, clients, and the public. This section covers the issues that businesses should be aware of with respect to employee use of the Internet. Guidelines are provided to protect a business from liability stemming from employee use of the Internet and e-mail.

DEFINITION OF AN EMPLOYEE

To determine how the law of the Internet applies to employees, one must first determine whether an individual is an employee. There is not always an obvious answer to this question, and the issues can become complicated.

Basically, employees are a kind of agent. All employees are agents, but not all agents are employees. There are two essential characteristics that distinguish employees from agents. First, an employee must be a human being as compared to artificial or electronic agent. Second, an employer has more control over an employee than over an agent. An agent typically has its own facilities and is independent. Also, an agent's services usually are in the nature of a single transaction, and not part of a continuing relationship.

Employees are distinct from independent contractors. An independent contractor is not an employee, and therefore an employer's liability for independent contractors is much more limited than that for employees. A worker is not an independent contractor simply because they are called an independent contractor. An improper classification can be costly. The key in determining whether a worker is an independent contractor or an employee is the degree of control a company exercises (or has a right to exercise) over the worker's performance of the work. The more control exercised, the more likely the worker will be considered an employee. The less control exercised, the more likely the worker is an independent contractor. The IRS Web site provides a helpful overview of how to determine whether a worker is an employee or independent contractor. See http://www.irs.gov/ plain/forms-pubs/pubs/p15204.html.

EMPLOYER LIABILITY

The ease at which e-mail is transmitted encourages informality and often reduces inhibitions. E-mail allows for the rapid dissemination of ideas, plans, and documents. Employees are frequently allowed unlimited access to e-mail and the Internet. This exposes the employer to many risks.

Employers can be subject to liability to third parties from actions of their employees. Such liability can arise from action of the employees done within the scope of their employment. An employer can be liable for sexual or racial harassment perpetrated or furthered by e-mail. Also, careless and defamatory e-mail may expose individuals and the company to litigation. Other problems for employers could arise where employees breach copyright laws by downloading information contained on other web sites. There are also risks that employees may disclose confidential company secrets to competitors or third parties.

The extent to which an employer is liable for employee conduct varies. Under the general concept of *respondeat superior*, an employer is liable for the damaged party's injuries if the employee's injurious actions occurred within the scope of the employee's employment. The scope-of-employment analysis does not lend itself to any simple definition, but courts traditionally apply the following factors:

- the time, place, and occasion of the act;
- the relationship between employer and employee;

- if the act is commonly done by employees;
- if the act departed from normal scope of work; and
- if the act was reasonably anticipated by the employer.

An employer cannot assume that it will escape liability merely because it does not know such action is occurring. A company will be liable if management-level employees knew, or in the exercise of reasonable care should have known about offensive conduct. See Faragher v. City of Boca Raton, 524 U.S. 775, (1998). Prompt action to remedy a hostile atmosphere may relieve the employer of liability, but there is no guarantee.

PRIVACY OF EMPLOYEE E-MAIL

One method of reducing an employer's liability is to monitor or at least have the right to monitor employee e-mail. There are limitations to the extent an employer may monitor e-mail. Statutes have carved out exceptions to allow a company to monitor employee activity where there is a legitimate business purpose.

The Federal Electronic Communications Privacy Act of 1986 ("ECPA") 18 U.S.C. §§ 2510-2521, 2701-2709, 2711 generally prohibits the interception of electronic communications, including e-mail. However, three major exceptions to the ECPA may allow the interception of employee e-mail. First, an employer can monitor employee e-mail where the employee has consented to monitoring. This consent can either be express, where the employee actually agrees to the monitoring, or implied, where the employee continues to use the employer's e-mail system after being expressly informed that the employer intends to monitor e-mail. (See Privacy section in Commercial Transactions for discussion of ECPA and related federal privacy laws.)

The ECPA also allows the provider of electronic communication services to monitor communications when the monitoring is a necessary incident of the rendition of services or of the protection of the rights or property of the provider. This exception allows an employer to monitor e-mail transmitted via an employer-provided system. Note that this exception would not apply to situations in which the employer simply provides the employee access to a commercial e-mail service.

Finally, the ECPA provides that the interception of electronic communication is lawful if it is for a legitimate business purpose. Courts have taken two separate approaches to this exception. Under the first approach, an employer may monitor e-mail where the employee has been informed of the monitoring and it is necessary to protect the employer's business interests. The second approach examines the content of the intercepted communication. Under this approach an employer may intercept business related e-mails but not personal e-mails. An e-mail message is considered business related e-mail if it is a message in which the employer has a legal interest or the interception is necessary to guard against the unauthorized use of the e-mail equipment.

A company will have a legal interest in an e-mail message when the message is either in pursuit of the employer's business or is a detriment to the employer's business. An employer that wishes to leave open the opportunity of monitoring employee e-mail messages would be well advised to inform its employees that it reserves the right to monitor e-mail messages. By informing employees, the employer will be in a stronger position to argue that its employees do not have a "reasonable expectation" of privacy in their e-mail messages and will thus avoid having to rely on the court's own notion of what privacy expectation is reasonable.

Courts dealing with these issues generally protect the company's interest when it is legitimate. Most courts have found that the interests of the company outweigh an employee's expectation of a right to privacy. It appears that an employer who wants to monitor employee e-mail can readily do so once that e-mail has been stored.

E-MAIL AND INTERNET USAGE POLICY

The best solution to limiting an employer's liability is to establish an official e-mail usage policy. This policy should be carefully conceived and disseminated to all employees. A physical copy should be given to employees and posted with other official legal notices to employees. Also, employees should acknowledge agreement with that policy.

The content of a company's e-mail and Internet policy depends on the type of business. Businesses with confidential information and trade secrets may want to have a stricter policy. The policy should be included in the employer's disciplinary code. The following is a list of issues that the policy should address:

- state that all e-mail correspondence is the property of the employer and employee e-mail is not considered private;
- state whether the company system can be used for reasonable private use or whether it is solely for business use. If connected to the Internet, state that it can only be used for business-related purposes;
- state that the employer reserves the right to monitor its e-mail system at its discretion in the ordinary course of business;
- state that the system must not be used to communicate highly sensitive, offensive, defamatory, or derogatory messages, which include, but is not limited to, messages that are inconsistent with the employer's policies concerning sexual harassment, equal employment opportunity, etc.; and
- state that all downloaded files from the Internet must be checked for possible computer viruses.

All personnel should use care when addressing e-mail messages to avoid inadvertent messages from being sent to the wrong address. This is especially crucial of confidential information. Development of a business/client address book listing all clients may reduce the tendency to inadvertently misspell an address. Businesses should also be cautioned not to use the "reply to all" function without first checking where the message could be sent. Proofreading an e-mail for accuracy and for the correct address will also reduce the risk of sending out private, confidential or inappropriate information. A sample Internet Usage Policy can be found at the United States Patent and Trademark Office website at http://www.uspto.gov/web/offices/com/sol/notices/fr990621.htm. Though this guide may be used as a reference, businesses should tailor a usage policy to their company.

STORAGE OF E-MAIL

All businesses should establish a policy for the storage of e-mail. E-mail does not disappear once it has been deleted. E-mail messages are typically stored in the company's backup system. Many casual yet potentially destructive messages sent over company networks and the Internet are stored in backup systems. If involved in litigation, discovery of computer data is available which includes the recovery of deleted e-mail messages and other information transmitted via the Internet or stored on a computer.

A company should establish procedures to control the distribution and deletion of e-mail. This will protect an organization from unexpected or inadvertent results in litigation. The following procedures should be considered:

- backup copies of e-mail should be physically separated from backups of the rest of the computer system. This allows e-mails to be deleted after a short period of time;
- any e-mail which the sender wants to retain should either be printed in hard copy format or else stored in the main backup system of the computer; and
- employees should be advised that e-mail will be deleted within a certain number of days.

EMPLOYMENT CONTRACTS AND NONCOMPETITION AGREEMENTS

A written employment contract should be used to specify the rights and duties of both the employer and employee. Contracts clearly define all the terms and conditions of employment and prevent future disputes. Employment contracts should be prepared with an understanding of how the law and Internet technology will affect the employer/employee relationship.

Many employers use written employment agreements with noncompetition covenants to protect trade secrets. Minnesota's noncompetition agreements are governed by case law, and, in this regard, Courts carefully look at the enforceability of such agreements in light of possible restraint of trade. Generally, for such agreements to be enforceable, there must also be adequate consideration. While non competition agreements are common, such arrangements are more prevalent among high-technology companies. It is essential for a company to include legally enforceable confidentiality obligations and to consider assignment and work-made-for-hire language concerning patents, copyrights and trade secrets. Minnesota also has a statutory requirement that employees be given notice of their rights to inventions created outside the scope of their employment without using any resources of their employer. See Minn. Stat. § 181.78, which provides as follows:

> "Any provision in an employment agreement which provides that an employee shall assign or offer to assign any of the employee's rights in an invention to the employer shall not apply to an invention for which no equipment, supplies, facility or trade secret information of the employer was used and which was developed entirely on the employee's own time, and (1) which does not relate (a) directly to the business of the employer or (b) to the employer's actual or demonstrably anticipated research or development, or (2) which does not result from any work performed by the employee for the employer. Any provision that purports to apply to such an invention is to that extent against the public policy of this state and is to that extent void and unenforceable.
>
> No employer shall require a provision made void and unenforceable by subdivision 1 as a condition of employment or continuing employment.

If an employment agreement entered into after August 1, 1977 contains a provision requiring the employee to assign or offer to assign any of the employee's rights in an invention to an employer, the employer must also, at the time the agreement is made, provide a written notification to the employee that the agreement does not apply to an invention for which no equipment, supplies, facility or trade secret information of the employer was used and which was developed entirely on the employee's own time, and (1) which does not relate (a) directly to the business of the employer or (b) to the employer's actual or demonstrably anticipated research or development, or (2) which does not result from any work performed by the employee for the employer".

Employee Laptops

On March 8, 2006, the United States Court of Appeals (7th Circuit) determined that a person who is provided a laptop by a company and who uses a trace removal software tool to erase data, may be liable under the Computer Fraud and Abuse Act [18 U.S.C. § 1030] even without an employment agreement or corporate policy prohibiting the use of such programs. See International Airport Centers LLC et al v. Jacob Citrin.

MISCELLANEOUS CONCERNS

LINKING

Easy movement from one web site to another is available through "links" between web sites. Hypertext links are the highlighted text, pictures, or logos on a website that, when selected by a user, connect to another web page. Deep linking occurs when a web site provides a hyperlink to another web site, but instead of going to the other web site's home page, it goes to another page deep within the web page hierarchy. The effect of this practice is that the linking site's advertising revenues may be enhanced by providing content from another web site, often avoiding any of the advertising on the other web site.

Litigation in this area has focused on three main areas: copyright, trespass and trademark infringement. In Ticketmaster Corp. v. Tickets.com, Inc., 2000 U.S. Dist. Lexis 12987 (D.C. Cal. August 10, 2000), Tickets.com linked to internal Ticketmaster pages and compiled that information on its own site to provide to its own customers. The court ruled that there was no infringement, however, because the activity fell within the fair use doctrine and the "hot news" exception. Likewise, finding that there was insufficient interference with the Ticketmaster web site, the court ruled that the physical harm requirement for trespass was not satisfied.

In contrast to the Tickets.com case, the court in eBay, Inc. v. Bidder's Edge, Inc., 100 F. Supp. 2d 1058 (N.D. Cal. 2000) found that trespass to a company's web server was a valid theory and granted a motion to enjoin Bidder's Edge from accessing eBay's servers. eBay is an auction site that lists millions of auctions each day.

Bidder's Edge developed software that searched eBay's server and retrieved information about the auctions. The court found the software effectively diminished the performance of eBay's servers and qualified as a physical harm under trespass law.

These cases show that Internet linking is an evolving area of Internet law that may implicate a variety of intellectual property concerns. Some businesses have actually entered into agreements to allow for, and control, such links between web sites. The American Bar Association has published a guide entitled Web-Linking Agreements: Contracting Strategies and Model Provisions, which is available for purchase at http://abastore.abanet.org/abastore/index.cfm?section=main&fm=Product.AddToCart&pid=5070311. The advice of counsel may also help a business evaluate the potential risks involved in linking and possible use of a web-link agreement.

FRAMING

Framing is another approach to keeping a particular business in the mind of a viewer. It allows the content of one site to surround or "frame" the content of a "framed" site, thus enabling a web site to bring up the content of the other website within its own display borders. Web users can surf through multiple sites within a frame in this manner, while the frame site continues to be displayed. Although there are legitimate uses for such a web page design, if the use of the frame incorrectly suggests to consumers that the information within the frame is somehow associated with the information outside the frame, then unfair confusion may result and liability may follow. In fact, with regard to unfair competition concerns, framing may be more objectionable than linking. See Hard Rock Cafe Int'l v. Morton, 1999 U.S. Dist. Lexis 8340 (S.D.N.Y 1999) (noting that framing, unlike linking,combines the websites into "a single visual presentation").

In addition to unfair competition, copyright and trademark infringement may be implicated with regard to framing. In Kelly v. Arriba Soft Corp., 280 F.3d 934 (9th Cir. 2001), the Ninth Circuit Court of Appeals found that a company's use of an image search engine that returned thumbnail-sized images was fair use but found that inline linking and framing violated copyright laws when applied to full-sized images. Thumbnail photographs are smaller versions of a full-sized image that have lower resolution than the full-sized image. Arriba developed a search engine that scoured the Internet to find images. The results page included thumbnails of the images. The court found that this action was merely a tool to improve access to images on the Internet. Because of the low resolution in the thumbnails, the court reasoned that the images would not be displayed in the same manner as the original. In contrast, the court found that the resultant full-sized images were not merely a means to access information, but rather, were the end product themselves. As such, the court ruled that it was not fair use and enjoined Arriba from further displaying the full-sized images.

DEFAMATION

Defamation is a major issue on the Internet, largely because of its widespread reach and its ability to conceal anonymous users. The basic issues underlying defamation on the Internet are almost identical to other areas such as television and the newspaper. Internet publication takes place when and where the offending material is accessed. Because defamation is determined by state law, the elements vary by jurisdiction. Generally, to prove defamation, a plaintiff must demonstrate (1) the statement was published; (2) the statement referred to the plaintiff; (3) the statement was defamatory; (4) the statement was false; (5) the defendant was either (a) negligent in publishing the statement and the publication was a direct cause of actual damage to plaintiff's reputation or (b) clearly and convincingly shown to have published the statement with knowledge of its falsity or with reckless disregard for its truth or falsity.

There are several areas where defamation can emerge on the Internet, including: (1) e-mail (including one to one e-mail, mailing lists and newsgroups) which can be forwarded to others, and (2) through the world wide web, including web pages and web sites.

E-mail from employees can be a concern for a business in which the company's name appears in the employee's e-mail address (employee@abc-co.com). A plaintiff may be more likely to sue the business, since it has deeper pockets than the employee.

The law to date has dealt primarily with service provider liability, in part due to their deep pockets. For a good overview of defamation issues involving the Internet, see Blumenthal v. Drudge, 992 F. Supp. 44 (D.D.C. 1998). This case involved a statement published in the "Drudge Report," available through America Online, accusing White House Advisor Sidney Blumenthal of covering up abuse of his wife. The court granted America Online's Motion to Dismiss because, as an Internet service provider, it was shielded from defamation liability. According to § 230C of the Communications Decency Act, "no provider or user of an interactive computer service shall be treated as the publisher or speaker of any information provided by another information content provider," 47 U.S.C. § 230 (c)(1). This case contains an interesting discussion of defamation concerns arising from publication on the Internet and makes a clear distinction between the original party responsible for posting defamatory messages and the Internet service provider who may serve as nothing more than a conduit for the dissemination of the information.

Two prominent pre-Communications Decency Act cases dealing with service providers are Cubby Inc. v CompuServe., 776 F. Supp. 135 (S.D.N.Y. 1991), and Stratton Oakmont Inc. v Prodigy Services Co., 1995 N.Y. Misc. LEXIS 229, 23 Media L. Rep. 1794 (Sup. Ct. N.Y. 1995). In Cubby, defamatory material was published on a forum provided by CompuServe. The Court held that CompuServe would not be liable, because it acted as a distributor of a forum edited by another party and not as a publisher of the statements. CompuServe argued in *Cubby* that it had no opportunity to review the contents of the publications before they were uploaded onto the computer. It is important to note that a distributor generally must have some knowledge of the contents of defamatory material which it distributes before it will be held liable for defamation. The test laid down by the Court in Cubby was whether the provider "knew or had reason to know of the alleged defamatory statements."

In Stratton, defamatory material was again published on the Internet and the service provider was sued for the information posted by its subscribers. Here, the Court found Prodigy liable as a publisher, not a mere distributor, because Prodigy exerted some form of editorial control of the information posted on its bulletin boards and it utilized an automatic software screening program. Unlike Cubby, the Court said that Prodigy was clearly making active decisions regarding the content of information published on bulletin boards. Prodigy was not successful at arguing that it simply could not control 60,000 daily messages posted through its service. The case is distinguishable from Cubby and post-Communications Decency Act cases however, in that it involved use of a former employee's unretired access code. As such, Prodigy could arguably be liable under negligence theory.

The parameters of defamation claims relating to material posted by individuals on the Internet are still a largely unsettled area of law, particularly as defendants are often difficult to locate, thus deterring many potential lawsuits. As such, this area of the law involves uncertain rights and potential liabilities for individuals and businesses.

CENSORSHIP AND FREE SPEECH

It is no secret that pornography is freely available on the Internet. The Internet has also been used to distribute "hate speech." The question of the availability of pornography and the distribution of hate speech on the Internet is no less vexing than the question of pornography and hate speech in the off-line world.

In reaction to the issue of children's access to pornography on the Internet, Congress passed the Childrens' On-line Protection Act ("COPA"), which was to go into effect on November 29, 1998. See 47 U.S.C. § 221. One day after COPA became law, a lawsuit was filed by the American Civil Liberties Union along with web site operators and content providers challenging the constitutionality of COPA. This challenge pits the First Amendment's constitutional protection of freedom of speech against the desire to protect children from exposure to pornography. It follows an earlier attempt by Congress to regulate content on the Internet through the Communications Decency Act of 1996 ("CDA") which attempted to regulate, among other things, the access of minors to "indecent" and "patently" offensive speech on the Internet. According to the CDA, it is a crime to transmit a "communication which is obscene, lewd, lascivious, filthy, or indecent with intent to annoy, abuse, threaten or harass another person." Portions of the CDA were invalidated by the Supreme Court in ACLU v. Reno, 117 S. Ct. 2329 (1997) as violative of the First Amendment. The invalidated portion made it a crime to send any "obscene or indecent" material on the Internet knowing that it could be seen by someone under eighteen. COPA is an attempt to cure the constitutional defects of the CDA. In this second lawsuit, ACLU v. Reno, 31 F. Supp. 2d 473 (E.D. Pa. 1999), the plaintiffs contended that COPA will have a chilling effect on what can be communicated via the Internet and that COPA:

(1) violates the right to constitutionally protected speech,

(2) is not the least restrictive means available to satisfy the government's interests in protecting children,

(3) is overbroad,

(4) prohibits even useful information,

(5) restricts anonymous communications,

(6) is too vague.

The district court agreed with the ACLU's contentions, granting a preliminary injunction against enforcement of COPA. On appeal, the Third Circuit affirmed, ACLU v. Reno, 217 F.3d 162 (3d Cir. 2000). The U.S. Department of Justice filed a petition for writ of certiorari requesting review by the United States Supreme Court. On March 2, 2004, the United States Supreme Court found COPA unconstitutional. See Ashcroft v. ACLU 124 S.Ct. 2783 (2004) discussed in the section Advertising and Children.

Efforts to regulate speech on the Internet face tough constitutional barriers because of the extreme difficulty involved in narrowly tailoring restrictions so as to avoid imposing overbroad limits on legal types of speech.

One option that has been proposed is adoption of a "kids" top level domain, in which adult-only sites would be prohibited from operating, and an "xxx" top level domain where pornography and other adult sites would be available. Registrations in the "kids" top level domain are already offered through the New.net Registry, although no measures are in place to keep adult-content out of websites offered at these addresses.

For more information see the following web sites of the organizations involved in the lawsuit against COPA; American Civil Liberties Union (http://www.aclu.org), Electronic Frontiers Foundation (http://www.eff.org), and Electronic Privacy Information Center (http://www.epic.org).

GAMBLING

Internet gambling violates provisions of federal law under 18 U.S.C. § 1084. This section prohibits the foreign or interstate transmission of bets or wagers or information on bets or wagers by use of a wire communication. For example, operating an off-shore sports betting operation that utilizes the telephone system within the United States is illegal, United States v. Blair, 54 F.3d 639 (10th Cir. 1995). As Internet transmissions are conducted over telephone lines, this is a potential area of liability for gambling service providers.

Internet gambling services are also illegal in Minnesota. Such activities include sporting events, lottery tickets, and simulated casino games. Generally, it is unlawful in Minnesota to sell or transfer a chance to participate in a lottery, Minn. Stat. § 609.755(2). Sports bookmaking is defined as "the activity of intentionally receiving, recording or forwarding within any 30-day period more than five bets, or offers to bet, that total more than $2,500 on any one or more sporting events," Minn. Stat. § 609.75, Subd. 7.

Engaging in sports bookmaking is a felony. Finally, intentionally receiving, recording, or forwarding bets or offers to bet in lesser amounts is a gross misdemeanor, Minn. Stat. § 609.76, Subd. 1(7).

The Minnesota Court of Appeals upheld jurisdiction against an out of state Internet gambling service provider in State of Minnesota v. Granite Gate Resorts, Inc., 568N.W.2d 715 (Minn. Ct. App. 1997). The Court found that because the provider had advertised on the Internet on-line gambling services and had developed from the Internet a mailing list that included one or more Minnesota residents, the provider had purposefully availed itself of the privilege of conducting commercial activities in Minnesota to an extent that maintenance of an action in Minnesota did not offend traditional notions of fair play and substantial justice. Therefore, the provider was subject to personal jurisdiction in Minnesota.

There is also a potential for individual bettor liability in Minnesota. In Minnesota it is unlawful to make a bet through Internet gambling organizations. Minnesota law makes it a misdemeanor to place a bet unless done pursuant to an exempted, state-regulated activity, such as licensed charitable gambling or the state lottery, Minn. Stat. §§ 609.75, Subd. 2 - 3; 609.755(1). As Internet gambling organizations are not exempted, any person in Minnesota who places a bet through one of these organizations may be committing a crime. Further, Minnesota law provides for forfeiture provisions related to unlawful gambling activity. It is the Minnesota Attorney General's position that a computer that is used to play a game of chance for something of value would be subject to forfeiture under Minnesota law. For the Minnesota Attorney General's position on the legality of gambling, see http://www.jmls.edu/cyber/ docs/minn-ag.html.

FILE SHARING

Since the personal computer was developed, computer owners have traded files amongst themselves through a variety of means. With the advent of hard disk technology capable of downloading and storing large files, music files such as MP3s became one of the most popular subjects of file sharing. File sharing technology, of course, allows easy transfer and replication of all files in the MP3 format, including those comprised of copyrighted material.

In the first file sharing case to reach a court of appeals, the Ninth Circuit found music sharing pioneer Napster liable for contributory and vicarious copyright liability as well as for assisting online users to download copyrighted music, A&M Records v. Napster, 239 F.3d 1004 (9th Cir. 2001). Napster was developed as a software program that ran on a central server as well as on individual computers. Users who downloaded the software were able to search music files on others' computers, transfer those copies, and store exact copies on their hard drives.

In MGM Studios, Inc. v. Grokster Ltd., 380 F. 3rd 1154, 1160, (9th Cir. 2004) the Court concluded that, unlike *Napster*, these peer to peer file sharing services could not control activities of users and therefore were not liable. The Court also found that the Grolester service was capable of substantial non-infringing uses.

On June 27, 2005 the United States Supreme Court issued a long awaited ruling concerning the peer-to-peer networks that allowed millions of individuals to download copyrighted music via the Internet. In MGM v. Grokster 544U.S.903 (2005) the Supreme Court found that manufacturers and providers of software or technology that allows others to copy songs may be held liable for the infringing acts of others who use their software for such infringing activities. The Supreme Court determined that it was not sufficient for the provider of the peer-to-peer network technology to demonstrate that the software was capable of non-infringing use. Even if capable of non-infringing uses defendants who operate such peer-to-peer networks can now be held liable for the infringing acts of individual end-users if the defendants acted with the intention or objective of promoting use of the technology to infringe copyright. The Court found evidence in this case that Grokster had taken steps to actively induce and encourage copyright infringement and was therefore liable for infringement. It remains an open issue as to whether a peer-to-peer network with substantial non-infringing uses and that is not actively promoted as a way to pursue infringing activities will be deemed a legitimate and legal program.

The *Napster* and *Grokster* cases provide guidance to businesses that are using file-sharing technology on the Internet. Software should not be designed primarily for infringing purposes. Businesses must also recognize that they have some duty in protecting a copyright holder's rights. These steps will legitimize file sharing and will allow companies the ability to share and exchange ideas in real-time. Neither of these cases suggest that the actions of individuals who download and copy music or film are not infringers and the recording industry has more aggressively gone after individuals.

SECURITY HACKING AND COMPUTER CRIMES

As the Internet grows into a serious business tool, security has become a major issue.

There are many security systems and products which can be put in place to ensure that hacking and other security breaches do not occur. In addition, businesses can limit unauthorized access and hacking by employees by implementing security policies regulating the use by employees of the company's network.

The first federal computer crime statute was the Computer Fraud and Abuse Act of 1986 ("CFAA") (amended in 1996). This act imposes penalties for the intentional "access" into "federal interest computers" for the purpose of committing certain types of criminal conduct. The statute criminalizes seven types of computer activities:

(1) the unauthorized access of a computer to obtain information of national secrecy with an intent to injure the United States or advantage a foreign nation;

(2) the unauthorized access of a computer to obtain protected financial or credit information;

(3) the unauthorized access into a computer used by the federal government;

(4) the unauthorized interstate or foreign access of a computer system with an intent to defraud;

(5) the unauthorized transmission of program information, code or command, intentionally causing damage, or the unauthorized access of a protected computer which causes or recklessly causes damage;

(6) the fraudulent trafficking in computer passwords affecting interstate commerce; and

(7) the intentional transmittal of any threatening communication in interstate or foreign commerce for purposes of extortion.

Any computer used in interstate or international commerce in the commission of the offense would be covered by this provision.

Amendments to the CFAA have been added to deal with the problem of "malicious code" - computer viruses, computer worms, and other computer programs that are specifically and intentionally designed to alter, damage or destroy files or computer programs. Federal law also protects the integrity or confidentiality of electronic communications. In 1986, Congress passed the Electronic Communications Privacy Act (ECPA) to expand federal jurisdiction and to criminalize the unauthorized interception of stored and transmitted electronic communications. There are some exceptions to the ECPA, which provide business owners and individuals access to stored communications. The entity providing the electronic communications service is allowed to access stored communications and the user of the service is allowed access if they were either the originator or intended recipient of the electronic communication at issue. In addition, the ECPA does not prohibit conduct which is authorized by the party providing the e-mail (business owner) and for certain governmental or law enforcement activities.

Minnesota has its own computer crime statute, Minn. Stat. § 609.87 et. seq. The statute is based upon the federal computer crime statute and provides that:

- Whoever intentionally and without authorization damages, destroys, alters, or distributes a destructive computer program with the intent to damage or destroy any computer, computer system, computer network, computer software, or any other property is guilty of computer damage;
- Whoever (a) intentionally and without authorization or claim of right accesses or causes to be accessed any computer, computer system, computer network or any part thereof for the purpose of obtaining services or property; or (b) intentionally and without claim of right, and with intent to deprive the owner of use or possession, takes, transfers, conceals or retains possession of any computer, computer system, or any computer software or data contained in a computer, computer system, or computer network is guilty of computer theft; and
- A person is guilty of unauthorized computer access if the person intentionally and without authority attempts to or does penetrate a computer security system.

EXPORT CONTROL COMPLIANCE

Since doing business on the Internet may involve global electronic transactions, it is important for businesses to be aware of federal export control regulations and to implement procedures to assure compliance. An individual should be designated with responsibility for monitoring federal export control regulations and communicating such information to the relevant staff. Distribution or license agreements should include provisions requiring compliance with the federal export control regulations.

Of particular interest are the United States government's regulations on encryption software. Encryption allows for the protection of information by converting plain text into unreadable ciphertext. While the use of encryption may aid companies in protecting things such as trade secrets and confidential company records, the extent to which encryption provides such protection is great, and the protected information can all together be lost if the decryption key is ever misplaced.

The Export Administration Regulations ("EAR"), implemented by the Federal Department of Commerce, impose certain restrictions on the export of non-military encryption goods. Generally, one must obtain a license from the Bureau of Export Administration prior to exporting encrypted goods. EAR addresses the specific issue of exporting encryption products over the Internet. Under EAR, downloading, or causing downloading, outside of the United States, of encrypted source and object code software constitutes export. While the government maintains that the purpose of encryption laws is to safeguard national security and aid in the investigation and prosecution of crime, they have been challenged by some as burdensome, anti-business, and in a recent case, Bernstein v. U.S. Department of Justice, 176 F.3d 1132 (9th Cir. 1999), the Ninth Circuit Court of Appeals found that encryption software was speech protected by the First Amendment and restricting its export was an unconstitutional prior restraint. The Court of Appeals, however, recently withdrew the *Bernstein* opinion and granted a rehearing in the case. Such action is a prime example of the uncertainty and change in this area of law, like others involving regulations that change from time to time, and may require the counsel of experts who are knowledgeable in the most current government position. For up-to-date information and assistance, you can contact the United States Department of Commerce, Minneapolis Export Assistance Center at 612.348.1638.

PRESERVATION OF THE ATTORNEY-CLIENT PRIVILEGE ON THE INTERNET

Among other things, the attorney-client privilege prevents an attorney from testifying against his or her client's interest based upon information provided to the attorney by the client. This privilege only protects private, not public, communications between the attorney and client. It is the obligation of the attorney to not knowingly reveal a confidence or secret of his or her client.

How is the attorney-client privilege maintained when e-mail is used for such communications? According to the Minnesota Lawyers Professional Responsibility Board, the attorney does not violate the rule against knowingly revealing a client's confidences by using e-mail without encryption to transmit and receive confidential client information. Most states have similar standards, though many suggest or require obtaining client permission prior to using e-mail for sensitive information, and others suggest encryption. The American Bar Association Standing Committee on Ethics and Professional Responsibility recently issued a formal opinion that a lawyer may transmit information relating to the representation of a client by unencrypted e-mail sent over the Internet without violating the Model Rules of Professional Conduct. It is still a wise business practice to obtain client consent before using e-mail and to use encryption whenever particularly sensitive information is to be transmitted via the Internet.

COOKIES

As you surf the Internet, you may unwittingly leave information about yourself at each site you visit. Your e-mail address, type of computer used, and the URL (Universal Resource Locator) of the site from which you traveled is information that can be captured by each site that you visit. From these visits, a host server can identify certain information about an individual. This information or "cookie" allows the web site server to obtain information about the visitor's preferences. The use of cookies has obvious appeal to online businesses that can derive valuable marketing information from anyone who visits their web sites.

DoubleClick is one example. The company received a patent on a "method of delivery, targeting, and measuring advertising over networks" from the United States Patent and Trademark Office. This patent relates to the process of depositing cookies onto a user's computer and relaying consumer information back to

DoubleClick. DoubleClick is enforcing its patent against alleged infringers. Meanwhile, several defendants argue that the practice of collecting personal information is an invasion of privacy. Amid the controversy, the Federal Trade Commission concluded that the company did not violate its privacy policy with its data collection practices.

Businesses who use marketing services such as DoubleClick should be aware of a new privacy standard called Platform Privacy Preferences (P3P). The technology is part of Internet Explorer 6 and allows web surfers the ability to configure their browsers to automatically determine whether a web site collects personal information. The software differentiates "first-party" cookies and "third-party" cookies. First-party cookies are set from the site being visited. Third-party cookies are set by marketers or ad networks to track consumer preferences. P3P requires that marketers and ad networks develop and post privacy policies that can be read by the browser or they may not be able to use cookies.

Although new technology is on the horizon to allow a user to set preferences, businesses should be careful when volunteering their personal information when visiting web sites. Completing the ubiquitous on-line questionnaire, they may not realize the extent to which this information may then be used and sold for marketing and other purposes. There currently are no specific laws and regulations prohibiting the use of cookies on the Internet. However, potential plaintiffs may argue their cases using the Electronic Privacy Act, the Wiretap Act or the Computer Fraud and Abuse Act.

SECURITIES TRANSACTIONS

The securities industry has already been profoundly affected by the Internet. The Securities and Exchange Commission (SEC) now allows publicly traded companies to submit financial information electronically. See www.sec.gov. The Electronic Data Gathering Analysis and Retrieval System (EDGAR) is a system that supports this on-line filing process. The SEC even makes available information on class action securities and fraud litigation. The Internet has also become a forum allowing potential investors to investigate and obtain information on companies. Actual stock purchases are now possible on the Internet. There is even discussion of possibly creating an entirely on-line stock exchange.

The benefits of easy access and the ability to process financial data on a global basis in real-time are enormous for those involved in the securities industry. Unfortunately, the Internet's ability to enable many people to publish and distribute information regarding securities and potential investments also results in easy access to false information. The flow and availability of information on the Internet is also difficult to monitor. There is increasing concern by federal regulators such as the Federal Trade Commission about on-line credit scams and deceptive trade practices as well as on-line investment fraud. There are also new technologies trying to address the situation.

One such technology is a Smart Card. Smart Cards are credit card-size pieces of plastic that contain an embedded micro controller chip. The cards are attached to a personal computer and contain software and hardware security features and can run executable code. With this technology, users of the cards are able to encrypt data within the public-key infrastructure. Businesses dealing with secured transactions should consider such a technology to prevent multiple-user access to a single account.

ACCESSIBILITY-AMERICANS WITH DISABILITIES ACT

In one of the first court decisions to consider the applicability of the American With Disabilities Act (ADA) to websites, a federal judge rejected a lawsuit contending that a Southwest Airlines website violated the ADA because it was not accessible by blind users. The judge ruled that it was up to Congress to specify by legislation that websites were a "place of public accommodation." Access Now, Inc., v. Southwest Airlines, Co., 227 F.Supp.2d 1312 (SD Fla. 2002).

HELPFUL INTERNET LINKS
1. UPDATES OF THIS BOOK

Updates of this book can be found at:
http://www.merchant-gould.com
http://www.mnsbao.com

2. GOVERNMENT E-COMMERCE

The United States government is becoming more and more active in placing information online. This gives Internet users the ability to access government records, find information, and file electronically. This section provides the Internet address to the most frequently used federal government sites along with a description of the site.

The Federal Trade Commission (FTC) provides information regarding consumer protection, business guidance and provides opinions regarding current business issues. The FTC can be found at http://www.ftc.gov.

The Patent and Trademark Office (PTO) contains information relating to patents and trademarks and includes searchable databases for both. The PTO can be found at http://www.uspto.gov.

The United States Copyright Office is on the web at http://www.copyright.gov.

The Internal Revenue Service (IRS) web site provides information relating to employment and taxation. The IRS can be found at http://www.irs.gov.

The Securities Exchange Commission (SEC) provides an avenue for publicly traded companies to submit financial information electronically. More information can be found at http://www.sec.gov.

Federal legislative information can be found at http://thomas.loc.gov.

3. DOMAIN NAME REGISTRATION INFORMATION

A list of all registrars accredited to register universally recognized domain names is available within the ICANN website, at http://www.icann.org/registrars/accredited-list.html.

A list of registry operators for top-level domains can be found at http://www.iana.org/gtld/gtld.htm.

A current list of country code domains and links to their registries is available at http://www.iana.org/cctld/cctld-whois.htm.

The WHOIS database contains a compilation of registered and available domain names. The searchable database can be found at http://www.networksolutions.com/whois.

More information on ICANN and the UDRP can be found at the ICANN website, http://www.icann.org.

4. OTHER DOMAINS OF INTEREST

The American Bar Association has information from time to time on Internet-related items. The web site can be found at: http://www.abanet.org/buslaw/catalog/5070311.html.

Additional information on the American Civil Liberties Union can be found at http://www.aclu.org. The website for the Electronic Frontiers Foundation is http://www.eff.org, and the Electronic Privacy Information Center has a web site at http://www.epic.org.

The Minnesota Attorney General's online site is located http://www.ag.state.mn.us.

Information relating to UCITA can be found at http://www.ucitaonline.com or www.nccusl.org. Opposition to UCITA can be found at www.ucita.com.

NOTES